Praise for *Dance Like There's No Tomorrow*

The introduction of Evelyn's book grabbed my interest right away! "I wish my mother would have told me the facts of life. I don't mean about sex. I mean the facts of life about living."

It's always assumed the facts about life are regarding sex but throughout Evelyn's story, she shows the many ways that she had to figure out how to live and sidestep criticisms and abuse.

I couldn't wait to read more and I ended up staying up later than my bedtime because I could not put her book down. *Dance Like There's No Tomorrow* is a classic story of growing up within a family that doesn't show or share emotions and how it feels to have to live not knowing if you are loved or not.

I think that the events and feelings she described throughout her life are fitting for anyone today to relate. I admire Evelyn's transparency, and willingness to be vulnerable with her audience. I also enjoyed her sharing the shenanigans (watermelons!)

Evelyn had a strong instinct to survive and her resiliency is displayed all through the book.

I am looking forward to more from this author.

—Delaine Shay, *Author "And Then, We Laughed: a Memoir of Hope and Healing"*

Evelyn Leite is a talented, accomplished author who has courageously written an autobiography that carries a message of triumph and hope.

She humbly and transparently shares her life experiences of growing up in the 40s & 50s using such heartwarming stories that take the reader back to their own often bittersweet memories where warm family traditions are mixed in with often painful, conflicting family dynamics. She reveals the vulnerabilities one's formative years can have on early friendships and spoken and unspoken family 'rules' that follow us into adulthood. It was hard to put the book down, drawn in by her rich descriptions that made you feel as though you were part of the story.

A wonderful excerpt of her memories as a young girl in South Dakota:

New Year's Eve 1953. We're celebrating by listening to Times Square on our new electric table radio that was Mom's Christmas gift from her sisters. We have Nesbitt's orange soda pop floats—a real splurge at five cents a bottle—and sugar cookies with sprinkles. Our hullabaloo is complete with singing Auld Lang Syne, a song my mother taught us when we were old enough to know what New Year's was. The shack with the bare wood floors almost feels like home.

This is a book you will want to be the first to get-timeless and authentically written-one you will read over and over again.

—Nancy Schuler-Schmidt, M.S, M.ED., LAC, LIMHP

In *Dance Like There's No Tomorrow,* Evelyn Leite writes "everybody has a story mine is just one of millions." Her telling of her story, however, is one in a million. The pages of "Dance," like the pages of so many of her other works, are packed with raw emotion. The frank, simple language she uses to tell her story will be recognized immediately by thousands of other women and men and, yes, children, who grew up feeling different, feeling that there was something odd about them—something they had to keep hidden from the rest of the world.

From the first page to the final paragraph, readers of Leite's work will find themselves saying again and again, "Yes, I feel exactly that way," and "I thought I was the only one." She speaks for so many others who traveled through life trying to be someone they thought would be "a better person," and the many others who found temporary, too often destructive, escape through alcohol and other drugs. Leite's words feel authentic because it is obvious she has experienced herself the chaos and the jumbled thoughts and feelings of a young woman trying to fit in.

The young woman she brings to life in "Dance" lives in constant turmoil, torn between trying to please everyone around her and wanting to simply tell the whole world to just go away and let her be. Anyone who reads this book will see quickly that Leite isn't just telling a story. She's telling her story—and she's telling their story, too.

—Terry Woster, Retired Reporter

Dance like there's no tomorrow

Evelyn M. Leite MHR, LPC

Dance Like There's No Tomorrow
Fifth book in the *Blood, Sex, and Tears* series.

Published by:
Living With Solutions
PO Box 9702
Rapid City, SD 57709
Copyright 2019 © by Evelyn M. Leite, MHR, LPC

All rights reserved. No part of this book may be reproduced or transmitted in any form or by any means, electronic or mechanical, including photocopying, recording, or by any information and retrieval system without express written permission from the author, except for the inclusion of brief quotations in a review.

Due to the dynamic nature of the internet, any web addresses or links contained in this book may have been changed since publication and may no longer be valid. The views expressed in this work are solely the views of the author.

ISBN: (sc) 978-1-7335409-8-8
     (eb) 978-1-7335409-9-5

Library of Congress: 2019918458
U.S. Copyright Number: 1-8690394621
Printed in the United States

Disclaimer

This is a personal document based on events which happen to people every day. They happened to me.

It is a story about alcoholism and pain, about faith and healing, and about joy and recovery. It is written that all people in the helping professions may gain insight into problems family members face when alcohol is destroying their lives. It is further written to bring love, hope, and inspiration to people trying to cope with a disease they do not understand. This book is published with permission of close family members. Some names and events are changed but the story is real and could be happening next door to you. Or in your house.

This book is designed to provide information about the subject matter covered. It is sold with the understanding that the publisher and authors are not engaged in rendering legal, accounting, or other professional services. If legal or other expert assistance is required, the services of a competent professional should be sought.

Every precaution has been taken in the development of this book to bring you accurate and up to date information. However, there may be mistakes both typographical and in content. Therefore, this text should be used only as a general guide and not as the ultimate source for improving family relations.

The purpose of this manual is to educate and enlighten. The author and publisher shall have neither liability nor responsibility to any person or entity with respect to any loss or damage caused or alleged to be caused directly or indirectly by the information contained in this book. The author assumes no responsibility for any liability resulting from the use of the information contained in this book.

If you do not wish to be bound by the above, you may return this book to the publisher for a full refund.

TABLE OF CONTENTS

Dedication	i
Introduction	iii
Preface	v
Chapter 1 — Trying to Fit In	1
Chapter 2 — Marcie and Her Mom	13
Chapter 3 — A Working Girl	17
Chapter 4 — Having Our Farm	25
Chapter 5 — Out on the Town	33
Chapter 6 — South Dakota Nights	41
Chapter 7 — Disappointments	47
Chapter 8 — Company	55
Chapter 9 — Family Troubles	59
Chapter 10 — Rodeo Time	67
Chapter 11 — Fighting with Dad	71
Chapter 12 — True Love?	77
Chapter 13 — Chosen	87
Chapter 14 — Sinking	97
Chapter 15 — Giving In	115
Chapter 16 — Back Home	129
Chapter 17 — Rejection and Salvation	139
Chapter 18 — Who Am I?	151
Chapter 19 — A Milestone	167
Chapter 20 — Prepare for the Future	175
Post Script	189
Author's Note	191
About the Author	193

Dedication

Dedicated with love to the entire senior class of 1957. All of whom gave me a reason to go on even though they never knew how much their acceptance meant to a blundering farm girl with absolutely no self-esteem. You gave me a reason to persevere. Also dedicated with special admiration and respect to Mercedes Laramie, Bill Fischer, Mike Sargent, Glenn Frick, Glenda Terbell, Jim Stirling, Larry Meisner and Sharon Lippert. All of whom I owe a debt of gratitude. Just so you know life now is wonderful.

Introduction

I wish my mother would have told me the facts of life. I don't mean about sex, I mean the facts of life about living.

Like just because a guy is handsome, wears a uniform, and has big muscles, a great butt, and a grin that makes girls swoon, doesn't mean he'd make a great husband and father.

Or when you're on your own there will be bills to pay—rent, lights, food, and car payments. And every time you get a dime, said car will need new tires.

Or living on an airman's pay will guarantee you'll be lucky to get one new dress a year.

Or that leaving the military causes even more problems because construction workers don't work when it rains.

I wish my mother would have known that "Love is patient, love is kind," doesn't mean ignoring the obvious. It doesn't mean turning a blind eye to your out-of-control children. It for darn sure doesn't mean you have to allow your husband to verbally beat you up.

It wasn't that my mother and father didn't love their children or get obedience from their children. It was just that most of the time we were utter miserable failures at reading our parents' minds. There was a horrible inconsistency in our house. It was a pride factor, an ignore-it-and-it-will-go-away factor, a how-dare-you-not-know-what-I-want factor, and a rise-above-it factor—all accompanied by a strong do-as-I say-not-as I-do rule.

We are Joneses. We don't whine. We don't cry. We don't need anybody. We are lucky. We are blessed. We are brainwashed.

All of the names in this book have been changed to protect the identity of those who are involved in my story.

Preface

Everybody has a story, mine is just one of millions. All of my books are filled with pain and facts that many families hide because of fear of being judged. It is time to realize addiction and mental illness are things that need to be treated not hidden. They must come out of the attic which is where they used to hide addicts and the mentally ill back in the old days.

When light is shed on these issues and the elements of shame are brought out in the open, then those suffering from fear, anxiety, shame, addiction and Post Traumatic Stress Disorder will find more help and more acceptance. It is in this spirit of openness that I present my experiences which for the discerning reader clearly delineates the progression of the disease of alcoholism—a disease that is no more shameful than diabetes.

Denial must be seen for what it is—a way to avoid the painful truth. But avoiding the truth, makes for a crazy making family experience and creates the very shame, and anxiety that denial is meant to avoid.

The disease of addiction creates a jumble of mixed emotions for anyone experiencing it or watching it. There is confusion, anger, hurt, fear, hostility and attempts to control. Nothing works as long as judgment prevails instead of education. If you do not have addiction and mental health issues in your family, then you know someone who does. Thank God that it's not you and learn all you can about having compassion for those who suffer. We can all make a difference.

Chapter 1
Trying to Fit In

It doesn't seem to matter to anyone but me that we are leaving the farm I love.

We are driving across the frozen countryside during our Christmas break from school. Cold air is seeping into Daddy's tired red farm truck piled high with all the bits and pieces, odds and ends we'll need for now.

When they can afford the twenty cents a gallon for gas, Daddy will go back for more stuff. He'll even bring Mom's prized crystal and the walnut sideboard buffet. *If this is only temporary why do we have to bring so much stuff?*

We kids squeeze ourselves into the truck cab as efficiently as possible, treating space like a matter of life and death. Mike, Bill and Ted are behind the seat, Bernie and me are jammed in front with Mom and Dad. All of us front seaters are getting jabbed, elbowed, and poked.

It's a long sixty miles. The knocking motor coupled with the screeching wind almost drowns out Daddy's booming voice. "Keep looking out the window behind you, guys. Make sure we don't lose anything."

We pull up in front of a shabby, no-color shack with small dirty windows that squawk neglect. Daddy looks at Mom with a pleading look in his eyes. "It's not much, but it's only ten dollars a month and we'll find something else as soon as we can."

Mom nods. "Come on kids. We've got a lot of work to do."

Inside the house we find dull brown walls, a bare wood floor in the living room, two bedrooms and a kitchen with shabby linoleum. This place has an outhouse similar to the one we left behind so that hasn't changed, but at least we have electric lights and running water.

First boxes to be unloaded are the canned goods—jars of canned pheasant, beef, pork, and garden vegetables. An old beat up kitchen table with eight chairs follows. Next come our clothes, a couple of mattresses, our broken down couch, and an easy chair. Finally, a couple of bedposts, springs to go under the mattress and slats to lay the springs on.

Daddy hands Ted a dollar. "I saw a grocery store a couple blocks back. Run and get us two loaves of bread and some ring baloney." Ted grabs the dollar and runs.

Store-bought bread is a real treat. I've maybe had it twice before in my thirteen years. Mom digs out the mustard and opens a jar of pickles.

By the next morning, the windows are washed and the plastic drapes are up. Clothes boxes are emptied into respective closets, the couch and chair positioned with rag throw rugs in front of them in the living room.

§

It's New Year's Eve 1953 and we're celebrating by listening to Times Square on our new electric table radio that was Mom's Christmas gift from her sisters. We have Nesbitt's orange soda pop floats—a real splurge at five cents a bottle—and sugar cookies with sprinkles. Four of us play Canasta, while the other three play with the new Monopoly game that we got for Christmas. Our hullabaloo is complete with singing *Auld Lang Syne*, a song my mother taught us when we were old enough to know what New Year's was. The shack with the bare wood floors almost feels like home.

We haven't met the neighbors yet but we are already familiar with Alfie, a harmless looking World War II veteran who walks by our house every day talking to himself and picking up cigarette butts to smoke. Mike made friends with Alfie right away.

Our two-week Christmas vacation is ended. A scared eagerness keeps me awake all night before school starts. *What will it be like here?*

Mom can't take us all to school. "You guys can make it by yourselves," she tells Ted, Mike, and me. "I have to take the little kids to the grade school. You have your report cards from the last schools. You'll be just fine." Bill is in the fourth grade, and Bernie in the second grade.

At the school, two blocks from our temporary house, we sign ourselves in as the secretary in the principal's office peers over our shoulders looking for an adult. All of our report cards are in the straight-A category. Ted is a sophomore, I am a freshman, and Mike is in the seventh grade.

"Look at that!" Ted points to the pickups sitting in front of the school with shotguns hanging prominently in their back windows. "Man, oh man!" His envy stands out like the neon in the windows of the nearby bars. This town is a historic mecca where the guys wear big cowboy hats and boots, even in school.

I'm completely unprepared for the "Yuck, a farm girl" attitude I encounter from the girls in my class. I climb behind a fake smile and try to be agreeable. The boys are friendly, which makes me even more unpopular with the girls. I'm learning fast that girls are petty, empty-headed, vicious, jealous, catty things who giggle. They act prissy, batt their eyes, and fluff their hair. *Not me*, I vow. Only one girl in my former life did this—my cousin Shirley, who Mom said to ignore because "She's not really a member of our family."

Before the weekend, Mom has a job across the river in Pierre as a waitress in the dining room of the Saint Charles Hotel. She's all excited. I hear the pride in her voice as she says, "I just applied to be a maid, but the manager asked me to be a waitress. I told him I've never done that before, but he said that doesn't matter. He said he can tell I'll learn quick. He offered me fifty cents an hour!"

The hotel is a grand expression of Mom's former way of life, only then she was the one being waited on. Mom tells us about the baskets of fresh flowers on the front desk even in winter, even in South Dakota where flowers have to be bussed in. She says there are elegant plush carpets, leather couches, and satin drapes that even smell rich. Bellmen in blue uniforms stand at attention near the carved mahogany check-in counter. She says the dining room is so sophisticated with white linen tablecloths, real silverware with soup spoons and salad forks, candles and flowers in the middle of every table. It sounds just like the movies.

Dad hates it that Mom has to work. I can tell because he sounds ashamed when he apologizes to her in one breath and says mean things in the next.

Mom is grouchy and snaps at me. We don't get along well that first month. I hear, "Pick up after yourself." "Get home right after school." "Take care of the boys." "Don't be so snippy," and "Turn that radio down."

I am so lonely. Being the new girl in a class of kids who've known each other since first grade is like being the little Dutch boy Hans Brinker with his finger stuck in the dike. I feel trapped.

My dreams of stylish clothes, wonderful new friends, and all the new opportunities I would have are dashed. There is no money. Mom's first paycheck brings a welcome change from canned pheasant, canned beef, canned tomatoes, and green beans. We were running out of canned goods anyway.

I'm not doing very well at cooking supper with what's on our pantry shelves. There's not even enough flour to make bread, which I actually like to do. Mixing up the flour, yeast, water, and salt is kind of fun. Throwing it on a bread board once it rises to the top of the pan, then pounding it down with all my might, is satisfying. Forming it into loaves and buns is a challenge, but oh, does it taste good.

Dad smiles when I put supper on the table. He knows I don't have much to work with. He tells the kids, "Be patient, boys. It'll get better."

I'm pleased that he's looking at the bright side. When Mom is home from work, she's wondering why the clothes aren't picked up and the dishes aren't done. She doesn't have time to mess with my worries of not fitting in at school or my fears of being an outcast.

Running in from school one afternoon, I find a note for me.

> Dear Evelyn,
> I want you to know that our move here is hard on all of us. We need you to help out as much as you can without complaining. So please stop being difficult. I love you and I know you can do better. Whatever is going on with you, rise above it.
> Love, Mom

I swallow feelings of remorse. Mom doesn't know how disappointed I am and how lonely I feel. I'm like a lost soul, but I have to show up at school every day, holding my head high.

Mr. Moses, a man in his eighties, is doing his last year as principal and there's barely a pretense of order. Kids come and go as they please. The first week a senior girl sitting in the desk next to me in study hall starts putting her books away. "I guess I'll go home and wash my hair," she says to me as she puts on her coat.

"You can do that?" My mouth slings open at the thought.

"Sure, they already took roll. Nobody cares."

I was pretty good at algebra when we moved here, but when I ask Mr. Moses to help me catch up he sneers. "Girls don't need to know math. They only need to know how to cook."

I can't relate to girls in my class. Clustered in little groups, they stand in the hall whispering. If I walk up, they look at me like I've just crawled out of a hole.

Mable is the ringleader of about six girls. She throws parties at her house where everybody is invited but me. I overhear talk in class the next day about how much fun they had. She can't understand why the boys in school like me, when it is clear to her that I am white trash. One day I hear her say, "There's only one reason why the boys like her. She's not a nice girl."

Instead of scratching her eyes out, I toss my head.

The boys are nice to me because I speak their language. Like all boys, they live in ignorant bliss of their own affairs. They have no clue how cruel the girls in my class can be and how they bully me. Not all of the girls are mean, but the rest of them are a glacier of quiet.

§

This town we're now calling home went through a hundred-year flood last spring. Damaged buildings with high waterlines sit everywhere. We hear stories of using boats to get around and no school for weeks.

The house we are buying sits right on the river and has been completely underwater. We see pictures that show only the chimney visible. The people who lived in this house before us understand the killing power of the river. When we hear the story of their escape it gives me goosebumps.

When the flood waters receded, it left the basement filled with silt. The floors are buckled, the walls are wavy, but the

$3,000 price is right for my wheeler-dealer daddy. Dad dug through the silt to find the furnace. He painted away the flood destruction on the walls inside the house. We are all looking forward to the luxury of an indoor bathroom.

Our house is on a short gravel street three houses down from a famous old west bar on Main Street. Across the street from us, about a half block away and attached to Dan's Café, is the Snake Pit, a wild 3-2 bar (the cheap, low-alcohol booze for those under twenty-one years of age. You can get drunk on it but it takes a lot more).

Our back yard is an acre of timber butting up to the Bad River that empties into the Missouri River. To get to the river's edge we fight our way through thick trees and massive undergrowth. The solid ice on the river makes great skating, even if we do it in our street shoes.

When the weather warms up we are awakened in the middle of the night by the terrifying sounds of ice crashing, colliding, exploding, and ramming down the river. As I lay listening to it night after night I'm filled with dread and morbid curiosity.

The federal project that brought us here is building the biggest earthen rolled dam in the nation that will tame the river. There will be no more floods—no more ice jams—but a lot of people will lose their land. I hear Dad and Mom talking about the poor people who have to sell their land cheap because the government wants to use it. According to Daddy, we are lucky to have a house at all as people are pouring into town daily to work on the dam project.

Daddy builds a bedroom on the back side of the house for the boys, big enough to hold two full-sized beds and a monstrous dresser. The room is hot in the summer and freezing cold in the winter, as is the bathroom that sticks awkwardly off the kitchen like a wart on a thumb.

Dad puts up a partition in the master bedroom to make a small bedroom for me. I paint it baby blue and put up the flowing white fluffy curtains from my old room. It's tiny, but all mine, except when company comes. Then I have to let whoever is visiting us use it while I move to the couch or sleep on a roll-away bed in the dining room between the table and the buffet.

Our walnut sideboard buffet is here now and a vision in the dining room, with Mama's prized silver tea service, along with the pink Depression glass cake plate on it. Family pictures in frames help the buffet look homey. A portable record player is perched on a side table, close to the buffet, and we have a small radio in the kitchen. We only have a few records but the 78s and 45s we do have get played a lot.

I've practically worn out my favorite, *Because of You* by Tony Bennett. When I hear it I feel such a longing I can almost taste it. I make up dance steps and swoop and sway until somebody catches me. I don't play it when Ted is around because he teases me.

"One thing about you, Bubs, your face gives you away—every time. Whatever you're thinking is right there for the whole world to see."

I'm embarrassed that my feelings are hanging out on my face. *I have to work harder to not do that.*

Now that Mom is working so much, coming home to a warm house smelling of fresh baked bread is a thing of the past. Much of the time the cold house with the shabby living room gets cluttered with coats, boots, and books. We plop ourselves down on the saggy flowered couch that sits along one wall. A couple of wooden office chairs from Granddaddy Jim's house are on the opposite wall with a tall floor lamp between them. The plastic flowered drapes that Mama says will have to do for now cover two long narrow windows.

Two spotted terriers that Bernie and Bill rescued from the dump join our family.

Sometimes I sit by the river hidden from the view of the house by the tangle of trees and underbrush. I stare into the water, breathe in the beauty and pour out my soul. Sometimes I swear I hear my name. No one is there. Yet in the rushing water or the rustling leaves I hear a distinct *Evelyn—Evelyn*. I'm mystified by the voices, but not scared, because Mike tells me he hears the voices too.

Sometimes he and I sit here together and talk. "Hey Mike, do you ever have times when you know what people are thinking?

"Do you mean like when I say something to someone and they say, 'I was just going to say that'?"

"Yes, or like when you go to somebody's house and they say, 'How did you know I wanted to see you?' Or 'I was just thinking about coming to get you.'"

"Yeah, it happens to me all the time. You too?"

"Yes. Maybe we're like mind readers or something."

"Oh well, maybe it happens to everybody," Mike says.

§

Daddy's a butcher in a grocery store now (something like the job he did in Custer). According to him, it's a good thing he doesn't have to work on the dam project. "Save that work for younger guys, even though they are making a ton of money." For a while he's home every night for supper.

His job wants him to have a telephone so they can reach him. It's a glorious day when the black Bell System rotary-dial phone with our new number right in the center, is hooked up and placed on its own small telephone table in front of the dining room window.

§

To please my mom and the punishing God who is going to hurt them if I'm not careful—I try hard to control my brothers' behavior. I boss them around and check on their activities. Since it's my job to keep the house clean, I pick up the boys' stuff and hide it. They can't have it back until they promise to pick up after themselves. This drama takes place almost daily.

"I need my coat. Where's my coat?"

"I don't know. Did you hang it up?"

"I can't find my gloves . . . boots . . . cap."

They grumble and grumble some more and sometimes I'll hear a swear word, but that doesn't move me. But sweet words do.

Ted always seems to know just the right things to say.

Chapter 2
Marci and Her Mom

I don't even notice Marcie at first, but the second week of school Ted spots classy, dark-haired, creamy-skinned Marcie. "See that girl over there? Find out what her name is and see if you can be friends with her. I want to meet her."

I sidle up to Marcie one morning while waiting for the school doors to open. "Hi." I smile and ask, "What's your name?"

"Marcie. What's yours?"

"Evelyn. Are you a freshman like me?"

"Yes."

"I'm new here. I don't know anybody."

The welcoming smile on her face is priceless. "I've been here forever. What do you want to know?"

"Want to hang out after school? We can talk then."

"Sure."

Marcie is everything I'm not—tall with short, glossy dark hair. She doesn't have to wear thick glasses like me. She wears cashmere sweaters and the kind of classy brown jodhpurs with tall, darker brown riding boots that Elizabeth Taylor wears in *National Velvet*. I wear homemade cotton dirndl skirts, saddle shoes, and cotton blouses. She has a parka with a fur collar while I'm still wearing Aunt Dorothy's old brown coat. She always has money to spend. I rarely do.

Marcie is as shy and timid as I am energetic and outgoing. In no time at all we're best friends. She doesn't like Mable either. Even though she's invited to her parties, she rarely goes.

§

Sitting alone in a pew in my Sunday clothes—gray checkered wool skirt and my best pink sweater, and wearing Mama's pill box hat, I catch curious looks from people who probably can't figure out if they should know me. Nobody speaks to me. The hundred-year-old Congregational church feels lonely on Sunday mornings, but it's better than being in the house without Mom. On the days she goes to work at seven in the morning I go and listen to the decrepit, gray-haired minister preach the usual repentance messages. I can barely understand his broken English and wonder where he comes from.

Three Sundays of guilt-producing, you-are-going-to-hell messages are enough. Sometimes I go with Marcie to the Catholic church her mother makes her attend by herself on Saturday nights.

Marcie and Allen are now connected like links in a chain. The three of us do most everything together except go to church. Marcie can't go to mine because she's Catholic. She says, "If I go to church with you, I'll go to hell for sure."

Ted says, "There is no heaven and where we're living now is hell."

I half believe him that we are already in hell, but I also believe that even if there is a heaven, I could never be good enough to go there.

Marcie and her family live in a comfortable upstairs apartment over the Bar they own. While their place is small, I love how everything matches in beautiful colors and looks expensive. When I stop by Marcie's to walk to school with her in the mornings, I sit on her fancy brass canopy bed or wait for her at the top of the stairs that smells of old booze.

Marcie's mother is a screamer and she's often screeching at her about not eating enough or not dressing right. "You don't appreciate the sacrifices I make for you," she yells. "You'd better hurry up or you'll be late for school."

Every time I hear her mother yell, I feel sorry for Marcie and grateful my own mother doesn't scream like this.

After school we hang out at my house, undisturbed by adults. Often, when Marcie and I are walking home, we see her mother clipping along across the street in her toeless high heels toward the post office or the bank. Marcie's mother is so glamorous with a beautiful, tiny, rosebud face set off with deep red lipstick, cascading brunette hair, and sparkling green eyes, usually hidden by sunglasses. She dresses in sexy clothes she orders from Frederick's of Hollywood.

One day we see her wearing her short fox fur jacket. She often wears black skintight leather capris and low-cut silk blouses. In her perfectly manicured hands with long red nails she usually has a Lucky Strike cigarette set in a gold-dipped cigarette holder. She wears diamonds, beautiful necklaces, and walks with a wiggle, which I immediately imitate. I watch her and long to be stylish like that, and to carry myself with such assurance, but don't think I ever will be.

She's so different from my quiet little mom in her simple and modest dresses, neat short hair, and sensible shoes. The difference between my dignified and genteel English mom and Marcie's fancy barmaid mom is like the difference between a Corvette and a Lincoln continental.

My mom often seems tired and underdressed in comparison. When Mom doesn't go to work at seven in the morning, she goes at noon and works nights, not getting home until after nine. At night she soaks her feet in hot water to deal with the blisters from working so many hours in bad shoes.

But when Mom gets ready to go to church or sing at an event, she wears three-inch, red, alligator toeless heels to compliment her high neck, long-sleeved black taffeta dress with a crinoline puff on the butt. This dress cost five dollars and ninety-five cents. It was my daddy's Christmas present to her a couple of years before we moved and it comes out for all special occasions.

Chapter Three
A Working Girl

I stay home with the little kids and the dogs most of the time. Sometimes Daddy is here, sometimes not. When I do get to go somewhere in the evening, it has to be with Ted. Daddy says, "You gotta watch out. You don't know what kind of riffraff is out there." He trusts my older brother to keep me safe from the scum—both young and old—who are always on the streets or falling out of the bars. Ted is my main companion and my bodyguard and I am his shadow—his partner in crime. He doesn't complain about having to take me, though sometimes he sneaks off without me.

§

A girl in my class is in 4-H and her mother is the leader. When she finds out I used to be in 4-H in Seneca, she invites me to join her group. This is someplace I can go without Ted. I go to her house for a couple of meetings, but I feel awkward and clumsy. The girls are all sewing skirts and dresses, but I've never done sewing before and the sewing machine is my enemy. I can hand embroider patterns on pillowcases, but that's about all. After a few times, I figure all this domestic stuff is not for me. I want a 4-H group where they ride horses and raise cattle but I can't find one for girls.

Debbi and Rose, who I meet at 4-H, talk me into getting my ears pierced. First, I have to find the two dollars for the gold stud earrings. "Anything but gold will make your ears infected," they say. Like my brothers, I hunt for pop bottles and milk jugs, and finally ask Mom for a dollar.

Once I have the earrings bought, Debbie and Rose come to my house after school, light a match to a needle to sterilize it, hold an ice cube behind my ear and plunge the needle in, first one ear and then the other. I'm dismayed to find that the hole in one ear is much lower than the one in the other. The studs are in place, no changing it now. "Use a lot of alcohol on your ears. Do not take the studs out for at least a month," Rose says before she leaves.

Daddy doesn't notice my impaled ears at first, but when he does, he snarls, "Oh sure, you gotta be like the rest of the trash. You better not ever let me see you wearing dangly earrings. Only whores wear those."

I'm still not clear on what a whore is. *Must be something pretty bad.*

§

School is out for the summer and it's time for me to get a job. I'm only fourteen but Mom lines me up as a waitress working at the hotel dining room. When she asked her boss Henry he said, "We'll give her a try."

I'm a little scared but excited at the prospect of making money. Mom brings a couple of black uniforms with their dainty white aprons home for me. The first day I just follow her around. The second day I'm on my own.

I have three tables to take care of and I'm doing pretty well until I spill a piece of watermelon in a legislator's lap. Tears come to my eyes. I'm horrified. As I try to mop it up with a napkin, he jumps up saying, "Don't worry, it's okay. First day on the job?"

"Second," I say miserably.

Now he's laughing. "It's okay; it's an old suit."

I feel like everyone is watching me and I want to climb in a hole. When Congressman Lawrence leaves with his friends there's a one dollar tip right where he sat. Every time he comes in after that he teases me. He'll say, "Got any watermelon around?" Or he might say to his friends, "Look out for her, she's dangerous." I look forward to waiting on him. When he walks out he always leaves a dollar or more on the table.

In the window to the kitchen there is a wooden block with a nail sticking out of it. When we have an order, we write it on a piece of paper and slap it on the nail. Sara, the cook, lines the orders up as they come in. She thinks I'm too young to be here. She quips, "You're barely as tall as this window. What makes you think you can be a waitress? Don't you mess up my food and make me look bad." For a while she even ignores my food orders, putting them up last even if they were turned in first. Mom tells me, "Ignore her and just be nice."

Maude, a wrinkled-up, pea-sized, eighty-year-old woman, is a long-time waitress. She has a tiny face with lips that would substitute as a can opener and she's almost bald except for a few scrappy gray hairs under the required hairnet (boy, I hate wearing a hairnet!). Maude knows who the good tippers are. When she sees them come in the door, she grabs water and a menu, rushes about, practically knocking me out of the way to wait on them even if the table is assigned to me.

Henry the manager, is a round, puffy little guy in a suit and tie who reminds me of a gnome. He has fat fingers and plump, fluttery hands, an oddly-shaped head with a patch of gray hair side-combed to cover a bald spot, and a fake smile.

Maybe he looked okay in his day.

He isn't bad to be around but we all hate it when his wife Verna comes in. She's a prissy-faced, proud woman who puts on airs. She'll stand there waving her hands with their long red fingernails and demand that some invisible crumbs on the floor or counter be cleaned up right now! When she and Henry come in for lunch or dinner together, I often have to wait on them because they don't tip and no one else wants them. Working helps stave off the gut wrenching loneliness I feel for the farm and my friends in Seneca.

One afternoon, I am trying to look busy—unnecessarily wiping off a counter for about the tenth time—when Henry comes in. He's a stickler for us looking busy. He looks at me and announces, "I want to speak to you in the back room."

A cold-sweat breaks out on my forehead and I feel butterflies in my stomach as I follow him. *What did I do?*

The back room is dark with one small dirty window high off the floor that lets in enough light to see the row of lockers where we leave our purses and coats. There's a tiny, smelly bathroom in the corner, and a row of shelves with uniforms, cleaning rags, new white aprons, and other supplies on another wall. Henry's big oak desk strewn with papers takes up much of the small room.

A sweaty Henry stands in front of me breathing hard and acting creepy. I barely understand his words. Something about my uniform being too big. "It doesn't look neat. Take it off. I'll get you another one."

The hair on the back of my neck stands up. I'm looking at the floor when Mom bursts in the back room through the big double doors that flap back and forth on their hinges.

"Did she do something wrong?" Mom demands.

"Ah, I was just going to talk to her about her manners." He moves to put his desk between him and her.

"If you're unhappy with her we can both quit right now."

"No, no, no, just keep her in line." He waves his puffy hand to say get out of here and we both go back to work.

Maude gives me a gloating smirk, her you're-a-bug-and-I'm-a-shoe expression. I feel like I've just dodged a bullet. That day I can't do enough for Mom.

After a while the cook likes me and starts calling me honey. She gives me tips on how to hold the plates just right, so I can carry more at one time. I can now line three plates up on one arm and carry two in the other.

Larry is a bellman in the lobby. He's a tall, thin, gray-haired guy with an infectious laugh. He looks so handsome in his blue and gold uniform. I like waiting on him when he comes for coffee or lunch as he kids around with all the waitresses. There's also a short fat bellman who reminds me of Micky Rooney and he's nice too.

My first paycheck is thrilling. Forty-five cents an hour is a fortune. I can buy shoes and school clothes. When I get to spend time with Marcie, I can throw around money on fifteen-cent hamburgers, ten-cent fries, and nickel pop. I also bought Marcie's pretty red parka with a red fur hood, her school coat from last year, for two dollars. She's getting a new one.

I like riding to work with Mom. We often leave an hour early because we have to drive over the narrow, rickety Missouri River bridge. If a piece of farm equipment comes across, we have to sit and wait until it's all the way over before we can go on the bridge. It's not uncommon to have six to ten cars waiting to cross.

My last day on the job is the Friday before school starts. When it ends, I miss that time with Mom, even if mostly we just talk about the boys and Dad. We both feel guilty about leaving the boys home while we go to work. She talks to me like I'm the other parent. "We have to get to the laundromat by Thursday, everybody is running out of clothes. The boys are going to need school supplies. Do you think you could pick up some pencils and tablets for them? Ted has to have a physical or he can't play football. Do you know what Mike's been up to lately?"

One Saturday four teenage boys from our former life on the farm come to visit for the weekend. We are tickled to see them as it's been hard leaving our friends behind. We ride around in Morris's car most of the day, showing them the sights around our area, just four boys and two girls (I don't do anything without Marcie) innocently enjoying a beautiful fall day.

After stopping at the A & W for hamburgers and root beer floats, toward evening we end up on a grassy hill outside town. There we notice a fenced-in contraption about six feet tall with lots of bells and whistles. Willie whispers in a stage voice, "Who knows what evil lurks?"

We all whisper back, "The Shadow knows." This is our favorite saying from our favorite radio show *The Shadow*.

"What do you think it is?" Morris asks as he shuts off the car engine. "Let's take a closer look." The boys tumble out of the car and climb over the eight-foot fence to explore the device and check out the instruments. Marcie and I watch from a safe distance as they climb around turning the levers and knobs. Then something breaks off in one of the guy's hands. He drops it to the ground. "Let's get out of here," one of them says.

Safely over the fence, Willie asks, "Do you think we broke it?"

"Nah, it was probably loose," says Ted.

Back at our house, we pop popcorn, play cards, and make beds on the floor for our visitors. As I go to sleep in my own tiny room, I can hear the guys laughing and talking. The next morning, before they leave, Dad gives them all pancakes and bacon for breakfast.

A couple of days later, a big headline appears in the newspaper—VANDALS WRECK NEW ELECTRICAL SYSTEM—with a picture of the contraption behind the fence displayed under it.

Ted gulps and asks me, "Are you going to tell anyone?"

"Are you kidding?"

Ted and I know we can count on each other.

§

Back in school, I'm now very aware of who my friends are. One evening Marcie and I walk to the elementary school playground to sit on the wooden merry-go-round and talk.

A new freshman girl comes up to us with her friends. She says something, I say something, and the bystanders start chanting, "Fight, fight."

I shrug my shoulders, respond, "What the hell," and punch her. She punches back, and we start wrestling. She's as strong as I am. She must have brothers too as she's obviously as used to wrestling as I am.

I'm only half-heartedly involved and I stop and say, "Hey, you're good."

"You too. What's your name?"

"Evelyn. What's yours?"

She smiles and says, "Dorothy." She's scrawny but kind of cute with straggly blonde hair.

"Shake hands?" I ask.

"Sure," she says and sticks out her hand.

I have a new friend.

Chapter Four
Having Our Fun

On a cold windy day, the kind of day that Dad always says is cold enough to "freeze the balls off a brass monkey," our old Studebaker won't start. Mom has to walk the three miles to work across the rickety old bridge and up the highest hill in town to the majestic Hotel.

Dad's upset when he comes home from work and sees the car sitting there. "What the hell's the matter with this car? I bet she flooded it."

He tries in vain to get it started. He's still working on it when Larry the bellman drives up, giving Mom a ride home after her shift.

A few nights later I wake from a sound sleep to hear Dad accusing Mom of having an affair with Larry. Dad is sobbing and acting like a nut case.

Trapped by the swirling, angry words, I lie in my bed trying to shut them out. Mom keeps quietly assuring Dad that he is the only man for her, and that she will never do anything like that.

The next morning Mom says to me, "Did you hear us last night?"

"Yes."

"You know it's not true."

"Yes."

§

Mom soon moves to being a night waitress in a steakhouse a couple of blocks away. She can walk to work. She's rarely home when I am, except she doesn't have to work Sundays anymore so we all go back to church with her. In no time we're sitting in our own pew, lined up like soldiers. I don't care much for church or the snobby people in it, but I like hearing Mom's beautiful soprano voice belting out *Holy, Holy, Holy* or *In the Garden*. My favorite is the way she sings *The Lord's Prayer* that almost brings me to tears every time.

During the minister's sermon Ted and I exchange eye signals meaning "This is a bunch of crap." Mom complains about the church women treating her like an outsider. "If you weren't born in this town, you don't belong," she says.

§

Dad knows nothing about what Ted and I are up to when we go places with our friends. Covered by the dark of night, we inch our way down the road without headlights to old Mr. Jurgen's garden to fill the back of a friend's pick-up with fresh watermelons. Those of us in the back of the truck throw them out on Main Street just to hear them whump, thud, and splash—and see the red stuff gush all over.

The cops ask my dad, "Do you know who's doing this?" When Dad relays this question to us, we shake our heads innocently. Dad looks serious. "You know Jurgens has a shotgun and he will shoot it at you if he can."

Don't we know! We watched him wave the gun as he took a couple of shots at the bunch of us hunkered down in the back of the truck.

I've made a few more girlfriends now, and they like to come over in hopes of catching Ted and his friends around. If the boys are there, the girls act like they really like me; if they are not there, they don't stay long.

"Wow, Evelyn, you're so lucky to have a brother," one says. "Look at all the hunky friends he brings home with him."

I have noticed this and a couple of times really try to get their attention but Ted's not having any of this. I'm just a little sister to them.

One of Ted's friends has a car. We pool our money to buy five gallons of gas for a dollar. If we don't have money, we use a siphon hose. We look for a lonely car, someone sticks the hose in the gas tank, sucks on it, and when the gasoline bubbles up into his mouth, he spits it out while shoving the hose in the tank. We have to be really quiet and careful when we do this. We roll up to the car with our headlights off and communicate via hand signals. When the siphoning is complete, we all get out and push the car down the road until we are far enough away to start the engine and race off.

Then there's always snipe hunting. One of our crowd invites a gullible classmate to go hunting and we drive him out to the cemetery on a moonless night. We pile out of the car, then walk around the graves a little before giving our victim a gunnysack and a flashlight. "There, I think I see one right over there," one of us yells.

The unsuspecting guy runs in the direction we are pointing while the rest of us run like crazy back to the car. As we jump in the car and peel off down the road, the guy will be hollering, "Wait, wait, wait for me," as he desperately tries to catch the car. We always go back for him before he drags the empty gunnysack too far down the road.

We hit the drive-in theater most every Friday night, with at least two people hiding in the trunk—so we all get in cheaper. Once inside the gate, we see other trunk lids popping open with two or three kids crawling out and dusting themselves off. As each car pulls up to a designated spot, you lift the speaker off a pole planted by each section and place it on the rolled down windowpane.

Two speakers to a pole place us very close to the car next to us. Neither car full of kids can do anything that the other car isn't privy to. If the grunts and groans of kids making out in the back seat gets too awkward, we get out of our car and walk to the concession stand, or just go walk around and enjoy the night in the open with the big movie screen hovering in the air.

After the movie, the gravel pit off the highway west of town is one of our favorite places to go. The first one to reach the top of one of the mounds of gravel screams, "Geronimo." The guys play king of the hill, but no one shoves me. I guess it's because they are afraid of Allen. Marcie is too ladylike to climb and prefers to watch from the bottom.

Bored with the gravel pit one late fall night, we're roaming around in unfamiliar territory, checking progress on the dam. It's dark with no moon to light our way. We're driving at a good speed when without warning the car goes flying through the air. It seems like we'll be suspended in air forever. Then, bam, thud, slam, the car lands upright on all four wheels. Four doors fly open and seven kids roll out.

"Anybody hurt?"

"What happened, man?"

"I didn't see that the road ended."

"We could be dead."

"How do we get out of here?"

"Get back in the car, we'll find a way."

Inching our way back to a main road, we are all absolutely silent.

"Don't anybody talk about this," the driver says.

Ted and I already know we won't be saying anything to anybody.

Back at home we hear Dad describing blow by blow the boxing match featuring Floyd Patterson, he'd just listened to on the radio to Mom, proudly displaying the money he won betting on this match. Dad loves boxing. He glues himself to the radio whenever a big fight is on.

When we were still on the farm, he bought two sets of boxing gloves for us kids as soon as we were old enough to put them on. He spent time showing us how to use them, and taught us the rules. "You meet in the middle, shake hands, never hit below the belt, and stop when the referee stops you. And you never cry if you lose." Now that I'm fourteen, I'm done with boxing but the boys still love it. Or maybe they just do it to please Dad.

As we're listening to Dad talk about the fight, I'm thinking about how we could have been killed tonight. I look at Ted and he's looking serious too.

§

Sometimes I long for the days on the farm when we weren't all scattered around like leaves caught in the wind. I feel like I'm losing touch with my little brothers and it hurts. Often the only time they talk to me is when I'm washing the dishes and they are drying. They have their own friends. When they talk around the supper table, they follow the family's unspoken rule of not sharing anything that remotely resembles a feeling.

It's way more relaxing when Dad isn't here—then we tell jokes and laugh a lot. The jokes are often at someone else's expense—mostly mine since I am the only girl. My brothers talk about their odd jobs like mowing grass or painting fences, or how many pop bottles they found to sell. Bill and Bernie met someone with horses they can ride.

Bighearted Mike has befriended a couple of disabled kids, who really like him and follow him around. Mike is the family whiz. He's smart, kind, and generous, and the pride of Dad and Mom. He makes up tall tales and keeps us all laughing at the supper table. He's a natural salesman and so crafty that he always lands on his feet. Dad often says, "I've never seen anything like the way Mike maneuvers himself into winning positions." He sweet talks old ladies who make him cookies, sweaters, and scarves, which he sells so he's never broke. He's always coming home with something new and amazes us all.

Mike and I confide in each other. He knows about the bullying at school. I know about his desire to be a scientist.

Bill is quiet, soft spoken, almost invisible. He never makes waves or complains. He's handsome with a chiseled face that looks like mother's, has her beautiful eyes and perfect nose. I think he's her favorite.

Bernie is a tough little cherub. I've always considered him mine to love, mine to worry about, mine to champion. I do my best to be there for him, but fail miserably when I try to stand up for him when Dad berates him over nothing, saying doing so will make Bernie tough.

At fourteen I am some kind of sight. My near-sighted blue-green eyes are covered by thick glasses. I have lots of freckles on a nose that seems way too big for my face. My five-foot-one- inch frame isn't very tall, but the muscles in my arms are as good, if not better, than those of a lot of the boys I know.

No one in my family ever says anything to me about my looks, other than once in a while Dad will say, "You look nice today." Ted will yell at me for wearing too much make-up. I spend a lot of time trying to get my reddish-brown naturally curly hair to behave, but it just won't. I try rinsing it in vinegar because Mom uses this on her hair, but it really doesn't work for me, so I keep it short. Some of the kids in school tell me I have a great body, and I admit I like the way I look in a swimsuit.

Ted is so very handsome with his wavy brown hair, sparking blue eyes, lean muscles, and slim hips. Mom is gaga over him. She says, "He's going to be president of the United States someday." Even I can see that's pie-in-the-sky thinking. But then she doesn't know what I know.

Once when I tried to tell her something Ted was doing, she said, "I've always told you to never tattle on your brothers. They have to be able to trust you, because the day might come when they really need you." So she doesn't want to hear about anything they are doing. If I was the mom, I think I'd want to know. But maybe she's right . . .

Dad will tell us we are worthless one minute, ("You damn kids are going to be the death of me.") and in the next sentence say, "I love my kids. I would die if anything happened to them."

I feel enormously guilty about leaving the boys home alone much of the time. I know they swim in the buff in the river behind our house because I go looking for them only to hear the voices of a flock of little boys hollering, "Get out of here. Don't come down here. Go away." They could drown and I wonder what should I do. In the end I do nothing. Dad's already told them to stay out of the river. Telling on them won't change anything.

Chapter Five
Out on the Town

Our area seemingly triples in size almost overnight. The town with its historic architecture is part old west and part booming new construction. The shift work goes on twenty-four hours a day. Sometime we stand behind the hedge in our yard at one o'clock in the morning listening to all the excitement downtown and the loud, raucous voices coming from the streets. We hear car doors slam, and the drunken voices of men going home, along with excited voices of those just finishing the swing shift and ready for a cold one or two or three. The overly loud jukeboxes from the bars boom out bawdy Hank Williams or Ferlin Husky tunes.

I don't much care for western music as there's always a broken heart, a drifter, and a whiny guitar. I much prefer Frank Sinatra or Bing Crosby. Rosemary Clooney isn't bad either.

The schools are bursting at the seams with new kids. I'm sure glad we got here months ago as some families have no place to live. Dad cuts down most of the jungle between us and the river to build a trailer court in our backyard. House trailers start moving in even before it's complete—new and shiny, shabby and old, and everything in between. Many of my new friends live in our trailer court.

Though it's been nice having some time to do what I want, it's hard living without money so I want to get a job at

Dan's Café. Just before Thanksgiving I catch a ride over to the hotel to ask for a reference from Henry. He isn't there but his wife Verna is. She's sitting in the dining room, at one of the linen-covered tables, folding cloth napkins for the evening meal. She gives me a condescending, critical look as I walk up to her.

I twist my hands together and ask, "I wonder if you'd give me a reference. I'm applying for an after-school job."

"I don't know if I can do that. Have you grown up any?"

"Yes, ma'am." *Easy, easy, don't let her see your anger.*

She raises an eyebrow. "I'll give you one but I'm not sure you deserve it. Who should I make this out to?"

"Just put To Whom It May Concern, please."

Bitch.

"Maude, go get me a piece of hotel stationery."

Maude sneers at me. No wonder she has to work here at the age of eighty. No one can stand her.

Verna scrawls something on hotel stationery while I stand there like a self-conscious lump, saved only by the fact that she doesn't know I know her husband is a pervert. I feel like telling her, "Oh Verna with the prune face, your husband likes teenage girls."

On the way home, I stop off at Dan's Café, which is only a block from my house where Dan hires me to work weekends and sometimes after school. Dan and his wife are no nonsense, all business, but tolerant and kind people. He cooks, she does the book work.

They also own the Snake Pit Bar. When I walk by the Snake Pit, it reeks of stale beer, cigarette smoke, and Evening in Paris—the perfume of choice for loose women. At least that's what my dad said when I brought the small blue bottle with the silver cord home from the drug store one day and he made me take it back and get something else instead.

On the afternoons I don't have to work after school, I stop to see Mom at her new job at the only department store in town. The other salesclerk treats Mom just the way some of the girls in school treat me. Mrs. Haggar is like a power-driven chainsaw massacre if anyone gets in the way of her commission. She's a strict woman, tall and wide, with hair pulled back into a bun, heavily powdered wrinkles, and rouged cheeks. She reeks of Tabu perfume—a heavy scent that makes me choke.

I think she's jealous of Mom because people like her. When I go in the store Mrs. Haggar gives me a don't-you-dare-touch-anything look. There are lots of beautiful things to look at—clothes I'd love to have. When Mom's busy I entertain myself by looking through racks of dresses, piles of blouses, sweaters, and stuff. If Mrs. Haggar isn't with a customer, she follows me around refolding everything I touch.

I hang around to talk to Mom, to ask her if she can go to coffee. She has no idea how much I long for some time with her. Mom always responds, "No, I'm too busy. Go home now, get supper ready, and see what the boys are doing." Mom usually works nine to six, but on Saturdays, it's noon to nine.

It's a zoo at our house on Saturdays with both parents running home for a quick supper at six o'clock and Ted and I fighting over who gets to use the bathroom first to get ready to go out with our friends.

A huge dance with a western band, usually Warne's Western Swing, takes place every Saturday night. I'm forbidden to go there but sneak in anyway. Marcie and I carefully plan our wardrobes down to the matching eye shadow. When Ted sees me, he screams at me—"Get that junk off your eyes! You look like a tramp."

Every Saturday Marcie and I starch our crinoline underskirts made up of yards and yards of netting material, hanging them on the clothesline to dry to tent size. I run around with pink wire rollers in my wild hair, hoping to avoid seeing anyone except Marcie. I sleep on the rollers at least four nights a week which is especially painful, but as Mom says, "You have to suffer to be beautiful." Marcie goes to a salon to have her hair cut and styled and she always looks sweet, perfect, and ladylike, while I've been told I look redhead-spunky and somewhat like a fire cracker waiting to explode.

Marcie gets dressed at home except for her crinolines, then comes to my house. We carefully put the stiff, starched petticoats under our poodle skirts, wear our sexiest peasant blouses, slip on ankle socks and white buck shoes that I use loads of shoe polish on three times a week to keep them sparkling white, and hustle out the door. We walk down the sidewalk with our rustling skirts taking up three feet of space around us—off to knock 'em dead at the dance.

The only problem is, we don't really know how to dance. So Marcie's mother puts money in the jukebox in the back of the bar and teaches us how to jitterbug, fox trot, and two-step. This is most fun when Bud, the slim, handsome, musclebound bartender has time to come back and dance with us.

Marcie's mother also answers our questions about sex or other curiosities in life. I think Marcie's mother is more hip than mine because she's twenty years younger. Once after such a gab fest with Marcie's mom, I go home and say to my mom "Why do you have to be so old?"

Both Marcie and I watch our weight closely. I'm five feet tall and aiming for a Marilyn Monroe figure. Marcie is five foot seven, a thin, beautiful goddess. I never eat until I'm full because I don't want to lose my twenty-two inch waist. My bantam rooster dad is one hundred and thirty-five pounds of steel, and my brothers are all lean and mean. Mom is only one size bigger than me. Marcie's dad is a short, round, good-looking guy, but Marcie's mother is all glamor and model thin.

Marcie and I practice putting on make-up and mascara. We do our homework in my room, drinking soda pop and eating whatever is available. One evening Marcie whispers so my mom in the kitchen won't hear, "Let's go down by the river. I have something." We sneak off into the thick trees, where she pulls out a package of Pall Mall cigarettes. It's exciting to hide out down there puffing away. Smoking fits in with our idea of being sexy rebels. Pall Malls cost twenty-five cents a pack so we have to make one pack lasts us for a week.

We daydream about leaving this town to have amazing futures. Marcie wants to live in a big city and be a model. I want to live on a farm and have six kids. *And when I do*, I vow, *I will love them deeply and never let them feel unwanted or unloved.*

We are the first girls in high school to wear boy's jeans instead of skirts or dresses—or baggy high-waisted girl's jeans. I got the idea from trying on a pair of Allen's blue denim Wrangler jeans. Twisting and turning in the full-length mirror, I like what I see. So now not only am I borrowing his shirts, I'm wearing his jeans too, which makes him furious. "Mom," he says, "make her take off my clothes."

All the girls in school wear boy's shirts—it's the in thing to do, along with wearing dog collars. Some girls wear dog collars around their necks like a choker, others wear them on their ankles. Right ankle for going steady, left ankle for available. Neck for not interested. The collars come in colors to match your outfit. I only have a couple.

Ted's low-waisted, butt-hugging denim jeans set off my figure in a way that actually makes me look like a curvy girl. At the western store I convince Marcie to try on a pair and she too likes what she sees. Boy's jeans fit us like the paper on the wall. The first day we wear them to school some of the other kids gasp out loud.

In school students pass around a spiral notebook called a "slam book." It's a secret thing passed from student to student when teachers are looking elsewhere. This day the slam book is full of remarks about the jeans we are wearing and one student writes, "Evelyn and Marcie think they're so sexy. Who wants to dress like a boy anyway?"

Another person wrote, "Well, they do have a classy chassis." That was good for a chuckle. Under Marcie's name is one word: "Sweet." Under my name is also one word: "Stuck-up." *I'm not stuck up, I'm shy.* Disguising my hand writing I write under my name "inferiority complex."

As we wiggle our little behinds all over town, we giggle at the wolf whistles and catcalls. Old Frank, a street vendor who sells comic books, cigarettes, and junk stuff, says, "I can see every pimple on your backsides."

"Don't pay any attention to him, Marcie, he's a dirty old man."

"Don't I know it." Seems he's propositioned her more than once.

Marcie knows how to bat her eyes and ask the dumb questions that make boys feel ten feet tall and bulletproof. I only know how to clam up and act tongue-tied or blurt out something stupid. Boys treat me like a sister. I listen to their woes, give them advice about girls, and treat them like brothers. Few of them ever see me in a romantic way.

I wish I didn't have to wear these horrible glasses. "Men seldom make passes at girls who wear glasses" seems to be true in my case, except for some perverts who probably don't really care what I look like.

Chapter Six
South Dakota Nights

I'm working as a waitress at Dan's most weekends and a lot of nights after school. Donna also works here. Her dad's a construction worker, and her mom isn't in the picture. Daddy doesn't like Donna because she's a high school dropout. He makes this clear one evening after supper. "She's a floozy, a tramp, and she's a bad influence on you."

"How do you know I'm not a bad influence on her?" I think it's so unfair for him to talk about my friend Donna. At this he throws up his hands, grabs his leather bomber jacket and hustles out, slamming the door behind him, his hat pulled down over one eye. Mom spits out, "Do you have to keep antagonizing him? Can't you ever just shut up?"

One Saturday night just after Donna and I get off work, we are standing talking in front of the café when a car pulls up and Ted yells, "What're you girls up to?" He and some of his friends have been riding up and down Main Street. The driver of the car yells, "Want to go for a ride?"

"Sure," we say and climb into the car. The guys are taking up a collection. "Got fifty cents?" Ted asks me. I fish fifty cents out of the tip money in my pocket and hand it to him.

Now that they have enough money to buy beer, it's time to find Billy, a slow man who's always on one street corner or another. "Hey Billy, come here a minute."

Billy leans his head in the car window. "What ya doin' kids?"

"We're rockin', Billy. How you doin'?"

"Oh, I'm just standing here waiting for some pretty girls to walk by."

"It's a nice night for that. Hey Billy, would you run in the liquor store and grab us a six-pack of beer?

"Sure. You got money?"

"Here's four dollars. Is this enough?"

Billy looks at the handful of coins and a couple ones that are handed to him. "This'll buy two six-packs and there'll be money left over. What kind do you want?"

"Grain Belt." The guys are in agreement about this.

"We'll be waiting for you in the alley behind the Snake Pit," someone tells him. We drive over to the alley behind the bar and watch people either stumbling out or being thrown out the back door. In no time Billy comes down the alley with the beer.

I don't drink because I signed a pledge during my confirmation in the Methodist church back home that I would never touch alcohol or tobacco. I'm already sneaking a cigarette now and then, so I figure I'd best pass on the beer.

Donna drinks so much she passes out. We want to save her from her dad's wrath so about midnight we take her to our house. Dad's just walking home from the bar and sees Ted carrying her in the house. Her head's lolled back, mouth is open and saliva is dribbling out, and her arms and legs are dangling like a dead person's. Ted deposits her on the couch as Mom comes sleepily out of the bedroom and Dad rushes in.

"What's wrong with her?" Dad asks as he anxiously hovers over the couch.

"We don't know." Ted shrugs his shoulders.

Dad is really scared. "Call a doctor. Call an ambulance!"

Mom's awake by now and asks. "Where have you kids been?" on her way to the phone in the dining room. She's dialing the doctor's number. Ted shoots a glance at me.

I take a deep breath and follow her. Just as Mom hears the doctor on the phone saying "Hello, hello," I confess. "She's drunk."

Mom sighs into the receiver and says, "Never mind." Turning to me she puts the phone back in its cradle and asks, "Did you drink?"

"No."

"Did Ted?"

"I don't know."

Back in the living room, Mom tells Dad, "She's just drunk."

Dad snorts. "Call her dad and get him over here."

When Donna's dad comes, he apologizes for the trouble, shakes Dad's hand and thanks him for the phone call. Then he picks up Donna's thin, rag-doll body and carries her out the front door. I watch from the screen door as he dumps her in the back seat of his car and drives off. Marcie doesn't like Donna. When I tell her what happened, she asks, "Why are you hanging out with that slut?"

"I don't know, I just like her." I know Donna looks tough but on the inside she's really fragile.

My friend Dorothy's mom is the night cook at Dan's Café. When I get off work at nine p.m., Dorothy and I sit in her mom's car parked in front of the café and watch people. It's a circus every night of the week and really crazy on Fridays and Saturdays.

Through an open door we see the Snake Pit is filled to the brim with boisterous, rowdy construction workers. Sometimes I see my dad in there. Often a tangle of bodies with boots a-flying bursts out the door of the bar in brawls ending in some bloody fights. There's always blood on the sidewalk in front of the Snake Pit.

One night we watch as two guys roll out together, the screen door flopping off its hinges. Then the guy on the bottom pulls out a knife and blood spurts everywhere. It happens so fast we can't be sure, but it looks like he cut the throat of the guy on top. The cops came and loaded both men up and hauled them away. Just another Saturday night in Fort Pierre, South Dakota.

Two former friends of my dad's from Missouri who had visited us on the farm a couple of times show up at our house. They have jobs on the dam and no place to live so Dad rents them my room. I sleep on the roll-away in the dining room for a couple of months. Gene and Johnny are nice soft-spoken guys with southern accents. Because of their work schedules they are rarely there when I am. Johnny, though, makes a point of being nice to me. He brings me little trinkets and asks if I'd like to go to a movie. I laugh at him like he's making a joke because why would I want to go to a movie with a thirty-five-year old man? Besides Dad would kill him.

Soft-hearted Mike often brings home stray guys who have no place to sleep to camp on our living room floor. One morning Mom is folding up a blanket after a guy leaves and out falls a Bowie knife.

He was sleeping fifteen feet away from me! Shocked, I ask, "Why do you let them stay here anyway?"

Mom says, "My family always helped people during the Depression. Someone was always at our house. Whatever we had, we shared. One time a whole family jumped from a boxcar and landed in our yard. Your granddaddy Jim let them stay for a month"

She gets a faraway look in her eyes. "They called it the dust bowl. You should have seen it. We'd hang clothes on the clothesline, dust would cover them. Then a swarm of grasshoppers would move in. Oh, and when we saw the sky grow black with grasshoppers, we'd run like crazy to get the clothes off the line. If we didn't get there before the grasshoppers hit, there wouldn't be anything left but rags and clothespins. They ate everything in their path."

Mom talks often about the Depression and the dust bowl, always ending with, "I'm so grateful God took care of our family." She tells me often, "Don't ever forget how lucky you are to be born in America."

When the guy comes back looking for his knife Mom hands it to him silently. I think she's still shuddering when she reports this to Dad at suppertime. Dad looks at Mike. "That's it, no more homeless guys on our living room floor. Maybe we should start locking the front door for a while." But the front door remains unlocked because Dad's usually the last one in at night.

§

Working at Dan's Café on Friday and Saturday nights is exciting because of all the muscle- bound, tight T-shirt-wearing, twenty-something construction guys who come in to eat supper. Some of them are really handsome and I have fun bantering back and forth with them. They make all the high school boys who come in look like babies.

Dan is a big easy-going boss who never gets upset. We have one drunken cowboy who comes roaring in yelling at the top of his lungs—not mad, just happy. He grabs and throws whatever he can get his hands on. When we see him coming in the door, somebody yells, "Here comes Jim." Then we run to rescue all the salt and pepper shakers, sugar jars, and napkin holders.

Dan takes him by the shoulders and in a soft easy voice says, "Come on Jim, I'll fix you a steak. You just sit down here now. Girls, get Jim some silverware and some water." We hop to it with two or three of us waiting on him. "Now Jim, you just sit here and be quiet, I'll be right back with your steak."

On the nights when Jim is just too drunk to sit there and be quiet, Dan walks him to the door, pushes him out and locks the door. Jim stands pounding on the glass until he gets tired and lurches away.

Chapter Seven
Disappointments

School is six blocks from our house so we can race home every day to eat lunch. Now that mom works nine to six, she makes it a point to be home for lunch most of the time. I sit across the table from Ted. We argue over fine points of history or current events or who sings what song. I like Elvis, he likes Hank Snow. He always has to be right.

Ted insists I've misunderstood McCarthyism. "It's about Communism stupid." In my frustration I flick a spoonful of mashed potatoes in his direction and it lands with a splat on his nose. A spoonful of green beans hits me in the face. Whoosh, I nail him with some cranberries.

Mom jumps up. "Stop this right now."

Ted's insulted. "She started it and she doesn't know what she's talking about."

"Leave her alone. You know Evelyn."

How I hate it when Mom uses "You know Evelyn" to explain my behavior. What does that even mean anyway?

Well, Mom, nobody knows Evelyn, least of all you! Maybe Dad would stay home if you would just be nicer to him. Sometimes he asks you to go out with him but you always say "No." Maybe if you'd go with him, he'd stay home more. Maybe our house wouldn't be so crazy if it wasn't for you.

§

Our school is in direct competition with the high school across the river but that doesn't keep the girls from our high school from liking the boys from that school and vice-versa. We make fun of the girls from that town, mincing around and mocking them by imitating the prissy way they walk and laughing at their behavior. They call us "low-rent" and say we come from the "wrong side of the river" but they have no problem chasing our male classmates.

When a roller skating rink opens up near the airport, teens descend like poor relatives at a BBQ. Since few of us know how to skate, everyone wobbles and falls, until they morph into swooping, laughing exhibitionists.

Those girls have their territory at the rink, we have ours. Noses in the air, they skate by us, making cracks and catcalls. Then we fly by them holding our noses.

The skating rink is where I meet Bob. He's a tall, gangly, yet graceful skater with the kind of craggy face that appeals to me. Bob's masculine manner holds out the promise of "I'm rugged and robust and I can take care of you." My first real boyfriend, he actually likes me better than Marcie.

He kneels on the floor, helps me with my skates, laces them up, manfully guides me to the rink floor and then teaches me how to swoop to the *Blue Skirt Waltz*. When the announcer says "All couples' skate," he races over and grabs me while other girls have to sit this one out.

It feels so good to be a member of an elite group of "wanted" girls. This is belonging such as I've never known. While we are dating, I can't have him come to my house for fear of Dad embarrassing me, so I meet him at Dan's Café.

We take in a couple of movies, do some hiking, and hang out at the café.

One Sunday evening just after Bob and I celebrate three months together, I notice a cute little blonde girl from the enemy side giving him a come-hither look. I feel helpless as I see him slowly shift without a word from me to her. Soon I am the one sitting out the couples' skate.

I feel like a wheel with a spoke missing and I don't know where it fell out. I study her. What does she have that I don't have? She wears a watch—I don't. She doesn't wear glasses—I do. She knows how to skate backwards—I can't. She's small, blond, and funny. I rarely crack jokes. If I even think of a joke it's twelve hours after the opportunity to say it has passed.

Now I aspire to do all these the things. I beg Mom for a watch, but the answer is no. "You don't need a watch until you're eighteen. Maybe we'll get you one for high-school graduation." Having a watch becomes an obsession with me.

At the roller rink I take off my glasses and blindly try to figure out where everybody is as I can only see bodies but not faces. I try to learn how to skate backwards. The first time I try to skate backwards my head bounces as I land, hitting the back of my skull full force. I look up to see people hovering over me. Somebody helps me off the floor. Ted and Marcie check to see if I'm all right. Usually I love swooping and swaying around the floor and losing myself in the music, but that night I sit on a bench in the skate room and wait for Ted to be ready to go home.

I have a gargantuan headache and a knot the size of an apple on the back of my skull. I take an aspirin from the medicine cabinet, kiss Mom on the cheek, and go to bed. I don't tell a soul about the big bump on my head. I get up in the middle of the night and throw up. When I go to school the next morning with what feels like a knife in my head, I can't see to read so I ditch school and go sit by the river.

The next Sunday I am out at the rink trying it again. I buy a bottle of Clairol hair color and the peroxide that goes with it. Maybe I can't be blonde but I can be smoky black and get rid of the red. Dad is furious when he sees my new hair color. I glare at him while he yells at me. "What the hell are you thinking? Your hair was a beautiful chestnut red. Now look at you."

When I look in the mirror I think black is definitely my color. *I look way older with black hair.*

Thankfully, Bob and his new girl stop showing up at the rink. It is a lot easier to sit out the couples' skate if I don't have to sit in abandonment watching them. Not that I *always* have to sit it out. Sometimes a pimply kid who can't skate well asks me to be his partner. I stop trying to learn how to skate backwards. I'm crazier about dancing than I am skating anyway. I always have partners when I dance. Big ones, tall ones, short ones, skinny ones—but few of them can actually dance.

§

At home I want to scream "Shut up, shut up, shut up" when I hear my parents bicker. My dad yells and my mom's quiet, soft voice defends herself.

Leave Mom alone, Dad. Mom, you're just making things worse.

It's even more confusing that Mom treats Dad like a king most of the time, baking him cakes, and buying him presents. And Dad tells us every chance he gets that Mom is the best wife and mother anyone could ask for and he loves her with all his heart. He tells us, "You'd better treat her right or you'll answer to me." The way they act just doesn't make sense.

Dad constantly throws jabs at all of us. I rarely know what he is talking about when he goes on one of his tangents. He corners me and gives me the third degree. "Where are you going? Where have you been? Who were you with?"

No matter what answer I give him, he says, "You're lying to me."

One of my friends has a face full of the ugly purple pimples. "Stay away from her. I know what kind of girl she is. Only sluts have pimples."

He's out of his mind! I think.

I'm bewildered when he acts proud at the thought of Ted scoring with the girls and when he teases Mike about his many girlfriends.

Then Ted drops out of high school. He shows up for lunch, acts like a cool cookie, doesn't tell anybody, just stops going to school. I notice I never see him in study hall anymore. I don't say anything to Mom, but as soon as I get him alone I ask, "Why aren't you in school?"

"It's a waste of time. I want to get a job and make some money." Whatever he does is right in my book.

"I guess that makes sense." Then I ask, "What's Dad going to say?"

"It doesn't matter, what he says, I hate school. I'm smarter than all the teachers and I'm tired of never having any money. It's almost Christmas, and I can't buy Marcie a present. I can't even buy a pack of cigarettes."

I give it one more feeble try. "Couldn't you work part-time like I do?"

His final words ring in my head. "I don't fit in."

Neither do I, I think, *neither do I.*

Ted is much braver than me. He has a mind of his own. I'm not allowed that luxury. I feel as if I'm punished because I have the nerve to actually think I'm a person. I'm caught in a muddle of confusion, constantly torn between love, hate, and I don't give a damn. Still, I try my best to rise above the chaos.

Ted immediately gets a job pumping gas at the Standard station.

Mom is doing that thing she always does with her hands when she's upset, rubbing her fingers, squeezing them together absently, while she sighs heavily at the thought of Ted dropping out of school. "Maybe he'll go back next year," she tells me.

Dad corners me. "Evelyn, talk to Ted. See if you can get him to go back to school."

I say "Okay," but I know it's not going to do any good.

Businesses are begging for workers. Ted could easily have two jobs if he wanted them. In addition to the drifters, construction workers, and civil engineers overrunning the town, we now have *those kinds* of women. There is even a house for them just outside town, and oh, the stories we hear about this place.

I first hear about this from Marcie. We ask a friend with a car to drive us out around the white two-story house that sits off by itself about five miles out of town. It looks innocent enough but some women stand at the windows and wave at us. We burst into giggles and urge the driver to "get us out of here."

Mom tells about the old guys bringing in these young women to her shop to buy them beautiful clothes. "You know old Virgil," she tells Dad. "He bought a barmaid one hundred dollars' worth of clothes today. Mrs. Haggar tried to make me share my commission with her, because she said she'd showed him some of the clothes a couple of days ago."

Dad shakes his head and says, "I wonder if the clothes are worth the price the barmaid has to pay."

Chapter Eight
Company

Holidays in our house are always an event. Christmas is the best, but Mom makes a big deal out of all of them. Valentine's Day she helps us build a huge valentine box into which she dumps a present for each of us. On Easter the Easter Bunny comes for everyone and each of us receives something new to wear to church. There's always a bounty of ham, beef, turkey, and molded red salad with bananas swirling around the top, and of course a lot of homemade bread, cakes, cookies, and cinnamon rolls. On St. Patrick's Day we eat green macaroni and cheese and drink green Kool-Aid. On Halloween we dress up like ghouls, goblins, and witches, go trick or treating and hand out tons of candy.

Family and friends come to visit us off and on all year long, but especially at Christmas. If it isn't Aunt Helen and her family, it's Aunt Pearl, or one of Dad's other sisters.

When they come, they don't see Mom cornering me and whispering, "Run down to the bar and see if you can find Dad. Tell him we have company."

I find him with beers in front of him talking to somebody or standing in front of a pinball machine with nickels piled up on the glass top. He methodically puts in a nickel, pulls a lever and watches the little steel ball swirl around and around until it drops in a hole.

When I say, "Dad you need to come home now. We have company," I see the rage in his eyes. The conversation is always the same.

"Go home. I'll be right there."

"Nope, I'm standing right here waiting for you." I'm filled with a sense of power and authority since Mom sent me. And besides that, I've been doing this since I was six years old. It's always the same. Except now it's a stand off. Dad tries to ignore me; I just fold my arms across my chest and wait.

Somebody in the bar says, "Hey Lon, is this your daughter?"

This always does it. I win. Swooping up his change, and emptying his glass of beer, he stalks out the door. I follow him feeling triumphant and guilty but I have done my duty. When he gets home, Mom breathes a huge sigh of relief.

Then Dad gives me the cold shoulder while he charms all the relatives. I often wonder if his sisters know him at all. Do they know about the bitterness that comes out of his mouth and chops our spirits into fragments and sucks the blood out of our dreams?

Chuck and Jean, Dad's cousins who used to visit us at the farm, show up. I don't recognize Chuck until he speaks to me in French. "Chuck!" I throw my arms around him while Jean laughs.

Chuck introduces a guy in an army uniform who is with them. "This is my son Jerry." Turns out Jerry is on his way home from boot camp and they stopped to see us on their way to Arkansas. I love Chuck and Jean, but I'm not impressed with tall, gangly, pimply-faced Jerry.

Ted and I take him with us on one of our watermelon tossing nights. Ted isn't home the next day when the cops come to our house. One cop walks in our living room and confronts me. "Are you one of the kids who threw the melon all over the street last night?

Jerry steps forward. "No sir," he says, "that was me."

I feel so ashamed. This guy I don't even like just saved me.

The cop looks at him. "You driving that car with the Arkansas plates?"

That's my dad's, sir," Jerry says.

"How long you going to be here?" the cop wants to know.

"Leaving tomorrow, sir."

"Well keep your nose clean or I'll lock you up."

Chapter Nine
Family Troubles

Dancing for me is like food to a starving monkey. The music entrances me. It fills me with a sense of walking on the streets of heaven, and takes me to another dimension where no one exists and pain disappears. There is only me twirling in delight on a moonbeam with one gangly teenage boy after another. One night the dance hall is full, my dance card is full, and I feel alive, full of life and optimism.

About eleven o'clock dad walks in—drunk. He pushes his way through the stag line that stands on the edge of the dance floor, shouting, "Which one of you SOBs is with my daughter?"

I'm horrified! Before I can escape, he walks over, grabs me, and drags me to the dance floor. My face red with humiliation, I pull out of his clutch and run out a side door, leaving him standing in the middle of the floor. I race home, sucking on tears of hatred, throw open the front door, and blindly head for Mom's bedroom where I throw myself on her bed.

"Do you know what he did?" I sob into her bedspread. "I'll never be able to show my face there again."

Mom is doing her nightly ritual of cold cream on her face. With a long weary sigh, she sits down on the end of the bed. "Now what?"

"I hate him. He embarrassed me in front of all my friends. He's horrible," I say, tears still pouring. "How can you stand to live with him? Why do you stay with him anyway?"

She moves back to the dresser and continues getting ready for bed. "Stop crying. You're just fine." Picking up her hairbrush, she starts on her usual hundred strokes.

Then she says, "For one thing you are not supposed to be dancing. For another I stay with him because he's my husband and God designed us so every woman needs a man. Besides, he never used to be like this."

God! God! I hate God too!

Dad bolts into the room. "Are you trying to make your mother mad at me?" He grabs my face in his hands and starts searching my neck. Mom turns to face us. "What are you looking for?"

It dawns on me what he's doing. "Oh, he's looking for . . . for . . . " I can't get the words out.

"Yeah, you know all about hickies, don't you? Why would you be any different from all the rest of the chippies you run around with?"

I jerk away from him. "Yeah? You won't find any hickies because there aren't any." *It's not likely that I'm ever going to let any guy suck on my neck until he makes an ugly red spot that everyone can see.*

I stand and glare at Dad with all the dignity I can muster thinking, *I wish you were dead.* Mom appears helpless, unable to react to the power struggle she sees taking place in front of her.

With his eyes blazing and his breath foul with the odor of rancid beer, Dad grabs me by the shoulders and shakes me until my teeth rattle. "You and your mother like each other so much, you just sleep with her."

This is your fault, Mom, I think. *Dad would stay home if you'd just tell him he has to. I could be in my own bed if you would stand up to him.*

I get my pajamas and move into her bedroom, taking Dad's place beside her. He moves to my bed for about six months, but Mom never says a word or gives any visible sign that she notices. I crawl into her sweet-smelling bed every night, inhaling the scent of rose petal lotion and line-dried sheets. I hang off the side of the mattress making sure never to touch her. In the morning I get up in silence and go to my room to pick out clothes to wear to school. My room is now filled with a man smell of tobacco smoke, stale booze, and Aqua Velva. Daddy stays in the bedroom with the blue walls and the white ruffled curtains until Aunt Pearl shows up one day and then we change places without a word.

§

Mom is sucking the life out of me. On Saturdays when everyone is home, she has a list of things as long as her arm for me to do. Iron the clothes, clean the oven, mop the kitchen floor. She tells me, "If you want to go to the movie tonight with your friends you better have this done by the time I get home from work. You can play when the work is done."

On holidays when all my friends get to sleep in and hang out, I have to wash walls and windows and go to the laundromat.

"When I grow up, I'm never going to do housework—or forget how it feels to be a kid," I tell my mom.

"Oh stop feeling sorry for yourself," she retorts. "You won't have any choice. Housework has to be done. It'll be your job to do it."

I look up at her from my position down on my knees, my hands deep in soapy water. "I'll get a job and hire a maid."

She's scraping wax from the kitchen floor while I'm scrubbing the walls. "Sure you will. Just remember 'Man may work from sun to sun but women's work is never done.'" Mom always has the last word.

§

Esther is a friend who I work with sometimes at Dan's. She's little and cute and has a great sense of humor, but she always seems sort of wounded. On the job, we find a lot to laugh about. There was the woman who walked out of the bathroom with her skirt caught in her girdle. And a husband who was in here with his girlfriend one day and his wife the next. Then there's Dan's wife who lets their kids destroy the place while we roll our eyes.

Esther dropped out of school as a freshman and no one seems to care where she goes or what she does. Sometimes I share my bed with her for several nights in a row.

One warm spring day when I get out of school, Esther invites me to stay overnight at her house on the other side of the river. I stop in and ask Mom if it's okay for me to spend the night with her and we walk the three miles to her house.

Her mom seems genuinely glad to see us as does Esther's younger sister, Lila June. Esther has been at my house for a week, but her mother doesn't even ask where she's been. Right away I notice a huge bruise on the face of her tiny little mom with her long black hair.

Their small, drab house is clean but the furniture is threadbare like ours, only worse. As we sit at the table eating beans and ham with cornbread, I can feel something sinister in my gut that I can't explain. I think her dad is acting strange.

Later while we are sleeping in her top bunk, her dad comes in and starts feeling around on Esther.

"Dad, get out of here, I have company."

Her youngest sister, Lila June on the bottom bunk says, "Not tonight, Dad."

What should I do? Just pretend I'm asleep? I ignore it.

The next morning, Esther says, "Dad, Evelyn needs to get to school and I have to go to work. Will you give us a ride?"

"If you're ready to go right now—I have to get to work."

"Dad, you don't work."

"Well, I have to go somewhere. Do you want a ride or not?"

Shortly after this, Esther moves to our house. Mom doesn't charge her room and board for helping with the housework and taking the laundry to the laundromat. Now lunch is ready when we come home from school at noon. We have clean clothes more than once a week. The windows are washed and I have help doing it.

Ted finds Mary Jane hanging out in the bus depot and brings her home. She's chubby, with blond ringlets that cascade down her back, and black circles under her blue eyes. She has run away from home.

"What are we supposed to do with her?" Mom asks Ted.

"Well, she ran away because her stepfather is doing things to her. She has no place to go."

Mom sighs and shrugs and lets Mary Jane sleep on the roll-away.

Mary Jane gets a job at the Ben Franklin, a nearby dime store. She lives with us for three months before Mom makes me tell her to call her mother in Omaha to come and get her.

"Her mother must be worried sick. You tell her she has to call her mother."

So when Mary Jane walks in from work I say, "My mom says you have to call your mother and tell her where you are."

Mary Jane looks weepy and says, "I don't even know if they care where I am."

I insist. "It's time you call or I will."

She digs around in her purse and hands me a phone number. I pick up the telephone and dial the operator and ask to make a collect call. When her mother answers the telephone, the operator says, "It's a collect call from Mary Jane." Before I hand the phone to Mary Jane, I hear her mother say, "Oh yes—oh God yes!"

When Mary Jane hangs up she tells me, "We have to go to Western Union. Mom is sending me money for a bus ticket." Ted takes her to the station and when he returns he tells me that Mary Jane said, "Thanks for everything."

Esther's dad kicks her younger sister Lila June out of the house so Esther asks if she can come stay for a while. Through it all Mom and Dad are kind and welcoming to these outcasts.

I don't like it that the girls see my dad's crazy behavior, the fights, and the chaos. When I say something to Esther, she just says, "It's better than where I come from."

One afternoon Esther and Lila June are cornered in Dan's Café by their dad and hauled off to go live with an aunt across the river. I miss them but it's sort of a relief to not have them here anymore to witness the havoc that runs rampant in our house.

Chapter Ten
Rodeo Time

It's rodeo time and Connie, Dorothy, Marcie, Sheila, Myrna, and I are sitting on the rail fence alongside the chutes. Hunky cowboys in tight jeans, boots, and cowboy hats are everywhere. Casey Tibbs, nationally-known champion cowboy, is our local hero and is riding both bareback and saddle broncs. Jim Shoulders from Oklahoma rides bareback horses and bulls and is Casey's competition. We're excited to see them compete.

The grand entry starts and cowboys ride in carrying the American flag, with trick riders in their spangles riding behind them. As the national anthem plays we jump down from the fence with our hands over our hearts while the cowboys doff their hats and wait respectfully until the anthem is over. The flag bearers ride at a gallop around the arena. The trick riders make a few jumps on their way out.

I'm green with envy. *I would have been a good trick rider. Why didn't I have this opportunity?* When I asked Mom to find someone to teach me how to be a trick rider, she laughed at me. I can ride a horse better than most people and I proved to her I could ride around standing up on my horse's back.

We can see the guys behind the chutes with their shirts off, jeans down, taping up knees, wrists, or rib cages hurt in the last rodeo.

A small plane lands in the back field bringing in some cowboy who didn't have the time to drive between rodeos. Time is money to a cowboy and the rodeos are often hundreds of miles apart.

Sitting on splintery gray wooden rails that surround the arena as close to the chutes as we can get, we drool over Casey Tibbs and the local bareback, saddle bronc and bull riders. We yell our lungs out when Willie, Bernie, Joe, and others come barreling out of the chutes. Every rider worth his salt has at least one huge silver buckle he wears proudly when he rides. Some have five or six of the coveted prize buckles. Though cowboys may have a hat that costs at least a month's rent, we can tell who the real cowboys are by the ball caps they wear when they're not riding. Only dudes wear cheap cowboy hats all the time.

We're wearing our jeans, tight-fitting western blouses, and handmade leather and beaded moccasins. None of us can afford cowboy boots, with the exception of Marcie, who won't wear them.

Saddles, gear bags, and good shirts hang behind the chutes. Beer is popped open and passed around. Cowboys pitch in to help each other. They help get the gear on the horses or the bulls in the chutes. Ropes and saddles have to be just so. We hear them saying encouraging words, wishing each other good luck, and telling the next bull rider what to look for. "You gotta watch that bull, he'll spin left when you come outta that chute and turn just as quick to the right. You gotta watch for that."

Fort Pierre has a rodeo most every Sunday in the summertime. The stands are full of people but we wouldn't be caught dead sitting in the stands. We want to be where the action is—and where the cowboys are. When Casey Tibbs walks by so close we can reach out and touch him we yell, "Hey Casey, good ride!" He smiles that sexy half smile of his and waves.

When the rodeo is over we walk from the fairgrounds and across the Bad River bridge. Cars move like snails. Some of the guys honk and ask, "You girls want a ride?" We wave them away knowing we will be downtown before they even get to the edge of the bridge. The thin leather soles on our moccasins keep us watching for rocks and broken glass along the path.

Once we reach the main street of Fort Pierre, we sit on the tall marble steps in front of the bank and watch the people from the rodeo drive by. Casey comes by in his blue Cadillac convertible, and waves when we scream his name. I'm not the only girl in this crowd who'd like to marry Casey Tibbs someday.

Chapter Eleven
Fighting with Dad

One Monday morning I go to meet Marcie for school and she is gone. When I get to school she won't look at me. After school I chase her down.

"What wrong with you?"

"Mom says I can't be friends with you anymore."

"Why?"

"I can't tell you."

For the next week I walk to school alone and forlorn. Confused, I watch Marcie laughing and talking with other girls. *Why has she abandoned me?*

Saturday morning I'm determined to find out. I walk up to her apartment and knock on her bedroom door. I know her parents will be sleeping in because they work until three a.m. She will just be sitting around waiting for them to get up.

I hold out my hands and plead, "Tell me, please. What did I do?"

"You didn't do anything. Your dad told my mother to keep me away from you. He said we couldn't be friends anymore."

"Why?"

"Because my mother told your dad she thinks I'm having sex with Ted."

"Well tell her it's not true. *I'll* tell her it's not true."

She drops her eyes to the ground. "But it is true."

"But we promised . . . We're going to stay virgins until we get married! We took a blood oath!"

I remember how we laughed when we each pricked our wrists with a safety pin until we drew blood and then held our wrists together like we'd seen in the movies. We chanted, "I solemnly swear that I will never have sex until I am married," and laughed so hard we almost wet our pants.

"It just happened and I like it." Marcie's arms are crossed in defiance and she's definitely not apologizing.

Clobbered with the truth, I sag into a discouraged heap. The reality of it is too much. Then I get mad. "My dad doesn't choose my friends. You and I are friends and that's it! I don't care what you've done."

Marcie seems relieved. "But my mom . . . "

"The hell with your mom. The hell with my dad."

The devilish glint she gets sometimes came back into her eyes. "Okay."

My respect for my dad is already swirling down the toilet and this clinches it. I walk purposefully to the store to tell him he can't choose my friends. I see him behind the meat counter talking to a customer. When I get up to him I smell whiskey and I can see he's wobbly. I walk out figuring what's the point? *My Dad drinks at work?* The realization is too much.

Back at Marcie's apartment, I tell her, "It's settled. Let's go to Dan's and have a coke."

She grabs her purse, and says, "Okay."

I didn't know Dad drank during the day, though I'd noticed his bizarre behavior coupled with outrageous diarrhea of the mouth some evenings when he returns home at six o'clock. He starts raising Cain with whichever one of us gets on his nerves first. He yells, "Why doesn't anybody ever do anything around here?" Or "You brats, you take, take, take, and never give anything back." His words are littered with foul-mouthed curses.

By now I'm not scared of him anymore. I often stand toe-to-toe with him fighting to clear my name—something no one else in our house does. Mom tells me, "Shut up and ignore him," but I can't ignore him. I just wonder why she put up with it. The boys don't bother to fight with him. They just find ways to escape.

It's one of those soft, breezeless fall days at the end of summer. Sun-kissed leaves lazily fall from the trees in front of our house. I run home from school for lunch as usual, the little guys running right behind me. The house smells like chili and fresh cornbread. I'm starving and out of breath from running.

I throw my jacket on a dining room chair and race to the kitchen. I want to grab my chili before Mike, Bill, and Bernie get in the door. Daddy is standing at the sink. *What's he doing here?* Mom is in the bedroom getting ready to go back to work.

While I'm scooping chili into my bowl, Dad makes an announcement. "I'm sick of your behavior. I'm sending you to Plankinton." Plankinton, the state detention center for wayward kids, is the ultimate threat for all misbehaving teens.

Why? My chili all of a sudden doesn't smell as appetizing. I start choking back sobs but tears run down my cheeks. "What did I do?"

"You damn kids are nothing but trouble, especially you. I'm just going to load you up and you're going to Plankinton." *Not reform school! Not the place where kids who aren't wanted are sent.*

Mom come out of the bedroom. He looks at her and demands, "Don't you have to go to work?"

"Yes, but I'm not leaving until I find out what you're going to do."

Holy cow, she's going to let him do it. Oh my God! I can't even count on Mom.

Dad is ranting. I'm a sobbing, blithering mess when a knock comes on the door. One of the kids opens the door for my friend Dixie to come in. "I was at my aunt's next door. I thought I'd walk back to school with you." She's looking at me hard.

I look at Dad.

"Go to school," he orders.

Dixie sees my tear-stained face but she doesn't ask any questions.

I sit through English class with a throbbing head and the brick in my stomach weighing me down. Who cares about nouns, verbs, and prepositions when life is bedlam ruled by anarchy. Sneaking out of school between bells, I go sit by the river.

Maybe I should just jump in. No you can't leave your brothers. Stop this now! Go back to school and walk home with Marcie.

Dad isn't home for supper. He's gone when I get up the next morning. He's not home the next night either.

After this whenever Dad mentions Plankinton I give him my venomous, drop-dead-you- despicable-worm look—the kind of look that says I'm not afraid of you anymore.

Dad hates the looks I give him. "She's sneering at me," he complains to Mom. "She spitting at me with her eyes."

It is the only tool I have. My wrath is an all-encompassing force and the object of my wrath is not just Dad—it's God too.

Why did you put me in this family?
Why don't you stop my dad's drinking?
Why can't you help my mother see me for who I am?
Why is there never enough money?
Why did I have to leave Seneca?
Who are you, anyway?

I'm still in touch with Joyce from Seneca. We write letters often, keeping each other up to date on the events in our life. I saw her last summer when Mom and I and the boys went home to the Old Settlers Picnic (the once-a-year hoopla with a carnival and a parade and a community dance).

I hadn't seen any one there for a couple of years, so I dressed up in my skintight knee-length skirt with the sexy slit up the back, and my sleeveless low-cut blouse. I wore a latex rubber girdle with the garters holding up my nylon stocking, and my two-inch white toeless high heels. I don't buy cheap shoes—these cost three dollars and ninety-five cents. The expensive girdle cost eight dollars, but no self-respecting girl or lady goes without one.

It was fun to see everyone from home, especially Glenn, Willie's older brother. He looks me up and down and whistles. "You really are a girl. I could never tell."

I did act like a tomboy when I lived there. I'm happy that he appreciates what he's looking at. Joyce and I have had a crush on him since the second grade.

Joyce invites me to come visit her over Christmas break. Mom says I can stay a week because Dad has business at the farm. When I get there, Glenn is working for Joyce's dad. He squires us all over Seneca.

One day we go to his mom's farm twenty miles away and spend the day helping Willie haul hay for their cattle in the freezing cold. We pitch the hay into the giant wooden hayrack, breathing in the fresh cold air. In the late afternoon we go back to the house with freezing fingers and toes.

His mom, Inger, and his little sister, Bella, have made hot vegetable beef soup, cut homemade bread into thick slices and baked an apple pie. We gobble up the soup, spread mountains of home-churned butter on the slabs of bread and demolish the apple pie.

When Glenn takes us back to Joyce's house, he kisses me good night before he lets me out of the car. Joyce runs to her room and when I get there she's gaga.

"What was it like? Is he a good kisser?"

Pretending that I'm not blown away by his gesture I say, "He's okay."

Dad comes to pick me up the next day. I wave goodbye, not only to Joyce, but to a way of life.

Chapter Twelve
True Love?

Home is a good place to be away from, especially on Sunday afternoons. Now that Marcie's mother won't allow her to date Ted anymore, she doesn't hang out at our house but we still go places together.

Marcie and I love hanging out at the state capitol building across the river. It's four stories of marble with a huge copper dome—a colossal, awe-inspiring colonial building finished in 1910. We usually meet four or five of our friends there. We sit in the chairs in the legislature and pretend to be spitting in the brass spittoons placed beside each legislator's desk. We walk the hallowed balconies that are positioned so we can see four floors down to the marble rotunda. We pretend to be on the jury and sit in the swivel chairs lined up behind the varnished mahogany rail. We climb the secret back stairways, put there so workers can escape their offices without being observed, and explore the underground tunnels leading to huge buildings across the street.

There is sort of a hushed solemn air about all of us as if the capitol is a living thing and, out of respect, we have to be quiet in its presence. We stare at the murals painted on the walls and imagine ourselves living in the 1800s and riding in the covered wagons we see in front of us. Some friends of ours show up to enjoy the building, and when they're done they give us a ride home.

I bounce into the house in a great mood to find Mom and Dad sitting at the table talking. "What can we do?" I hear Mom say.

"Hell, I don't know. He'll come back when he gets ready."

"Evelyn," Mom asks me. "Did Ted say anything to you about where he is?"

"No, I haven't seen him for a couple of days."

"Did he talk to you about running away?"

"No. Did he run away?"

"We think he might have."

Ted comes back two weeks later. We're all thrilled to see him. Mom says, "Oh thank God! I've been so worried."

Dad says, "Evelyn talk to Ted. You're the only one he listens to. Find out why he left and where he's been."

"Where you been?" I ask Ted.

"Oh me and some guys just drove over to Montana."

"Why?"

"I just wanted to get away from this zoo for a while."

When I tell Donna at work what's happening with Ted, she tells me stories of what it's like to live in California. "Why don't we run away and go to California where my mom is?" Donna says. She's mentioned this to me before, and from time to time I've toyed with the idea. But now when I see Mom's face and hear Dad's agony at not knowing Ted's whereabouts, I just can't do this to them.

Ted's friend Pete is sitting in the living room with Ted one spring afternoon when I come in from school. He's

Esther's brother and is charming, with dark hair, green eyes, and the kind of craggy, masculine face I like. He talks to me like a real person and Ted doesn't object.

I'm sixteen now and I develop a huge crush on Pete. I don't care that he's a lot older than me. He once worked in the same gas station as Ted but now he's on leave from the army. He tries to make it a joke about where he's headed saying, "It's thirty days before I get to go to the hellhole of Korea," but it falls flat.

Pete hangs out at our house a lot. Marcie and I both like older men and I think boys in high school can't hold a candle to him. When I see pictures of him in uniform it makes me feel weak.

Dad, of course, doesn't allow me to date, but since Pete hangs around all the time, it's not a date. It's me going with him and Ted to wherever they are going. Marcie meets us on the corner where her mom can't see her get in our car. We go to the movies, the gravel pit, the monument on the hill where two French trappers traveling with Lewis and Clark buried a plaque. We end up parking on some dark gravel road away from other people doing the same thing we are — looking for a place to neck in private.

Pete tries everything to have sex with me. In the backseat of Ted's car, the long, slow kisses make my yearning intense. The heat rises up from my groin and has a mind of its own. Intense warmth fills my chest so my breath comes in short ragged bursts every time he kisses me. He pushes, I resist. I continually move his hands away from the places he's not supposed to touch. Finally I tell him, "Either stop trying to feel me up or I'm not doing this anymore."

Pete's response takes my breath away. He looks at me earnestly and says, "I love you, baby. I'd die for you. I love you so much I can't see straight. Will you marry me?"

I'm blown away. "Me, marry you?" I gasp.

"Yes, will you?"

"Yes! A thousand times yes."

Later I tell Mom, "Pete asked me to marry him! I'm engaged—we're engaged!"

"That's nice dear," she responds in her best if-I-ignore-this-it-will-go-away manner. *That's nice?*

Pete and I are riding in the back seat of the car in the moonlight. We just came from seeing Marlon Brando in *On the Waterfront*. Not my kind of movie, but the guys liked it. I look at Pete and think Pete has some of Marlon Brando's tough good looks. Ted pulls the car off the road and reaches for Marcie. In the back seat we do the same. After about twenty minutes, Ted and Marcie must be embarrassed by Pete's groaning, moaning, and breathing hard, and decide to take a walk.

I'm pulling away from Pete and continually moving his hands to a respectable place on my body. Pete stops for a moment and says, "You know, sweetheart, now that we are engaged we can have sex." I'm hot blooded—I'm panting, I want this.

But I stubbornly determine to stick to my vow. "Not tonight. Not this way." He jumps out of the car and walks off his distress. I suffer with my longing and settle for soaking up the thrill of being engaged to somebody who looks a lot like Marlon Brando.

The drive home is quiet. The next night Pete kisses me good-bye at the train station and leaves to go back to Korea, waving to me and Marcie and Ted through the train window as he slides past.

In a few weeks I get a letter from him on US Army stationery.

> Dear Evelyn,
> I really enjoyed the time we spent together this summer. You are a nice girl. Too nice for me. Marriage really isn't in the cards for me right now. I haven't sown all my wild oats yet. Tell Ted Hi for me.
>
> See you around.
> Pete

I show Mom the letter without saying a word. She reads it and hands it back. "Oh well, there are a lot of fish in the sea."

I go to school but openly mope my way through my days. One night when we are doing the supper dishes Mom confronts me. "Stop wearing your heart on your sleeve. Don't let anybody know you care."

That night when they are in bed I hear Dad telling Mom he is really glad the thing with Pete blew over. *I didn't even know he knew.* Marcie is the only one who seems to understand the disappointment I feel over Pete's rejection. Ted is noncommittal—doesn't ask any questions, say anything nasty, or tease me.

Though Mom is oblivious to what I am doing most of the time, she is very aware that almost every month some girl is missing from school. Because she works in the store with the public, she hears all the whispers about girls having to go away to an unwed mother's home.

Boys never have to drop out of school, only the girls leave in disgrace. But sometimes boys are forced to get married. Shotgun weddings are the topic of a lot of jokes and laughter, but they are not funny. Judy, a fourteen-year-old freshman I barely know, is forced by her parents to marry fifteen-year-old Darry. He has to quit school to go to work. She has to quit to be a wife and mother.

A tall, good-looking sixteen year old basketball star is forced to marry the sophomore girl he gets pregnant. She has to leave school, but of course he doesn't. Fifteen-year old Darlene and her boyfriend Lennie elope.

Mom and Dad are sitting at the table drinking coffee and talking about Darlene. When she and Lennie got back, her parents had the marriage annulled. Mom shakes her head over what a disappointment Darlene is to her parents.

Mom says, "I would never do that. If Evelyn ran away and got married, I'd let it stand."

Dad seems shaken by this statement. "Don't tell her that, she'll do it."

Is that what you want me to do, Mom, so you won't have to worry about me getting pregnant and shaming you the way Aunt Helen did?

§

Through the window in the front door I can see Mom sitting in her green recliner, reading the Bible. Dorothy,

Myrna, Sheila and I walk in. "Mom, can I stay all night with Dorothy?"

Dorothy stands there nodding her head up and down as Mom looks up from her reading.

"Yes, if you promise me you'll go right home and not be out running around."

"I promise."

Back to the street we go, liberated and independent of home rule.

Now we need a car. Nobody knows how to drive but I think I can do it. *How hard can it be?* We go first to Dan's Café to talk to Dorothy's mom, Edna, the cook. I put on my most sincere look and tell Edna, "I know how to drive." She fishes her keys out of her purse and reminds us that we'll have to pick her up when she gets off work at six in the morning. We pile in the car and I careen down the streets, trying to avoid oncoming traffic. Finally I drive us out to a country road so I can practice. I learn to drive with the help of a car full of screaming girls.

We find boys we know hanging out on the streets. "Want to come to a party at Dorothy's house?" We yell from the car windows. They show up with beer, pop, and potato chips. We crank up the record player and dance to Elvis Presley, the Four Aces, the Crew Cuts and some of her mom's old forties music by Dinah Shore and Perry Como.

On a hot July Sunday afternoon, Marcie and I are walking toward Dan's Café for a coke. A long, fancy car pulls up beside us. Chuck and Ed, senior-class football stars from the school across the river are cruising in Chuck's dad's new car. We are thrilled to be noticed by them, so we stop and flirt with them for a while. Marcie is a master at flirting, flinging her hair, pouting in all the right places, and cracking jokes. I mostly just stand there with a silly grin on my freckled face.

"You beautiful girls want to go for a ride?"

"Sure."

"Hop in."

Marcie climbs in the front seat with Chuck and I slide in the backseat with Ed, noting the new smell of the plush, tan leather seats. Close up, Ed isn't all that good looking with his shock of corn-silk hair and his too small eyes. I am searching for things to talk to him about but he doesn't seem all that interested in talking so we mostly listen to the banter coming from the front seat.

The four of us drive around town for a while, eventually heading out to the country. Chuck takes us to the Big Island Lake about ten miles east of town and pulls up in a secluded spot under the cool shade of a stand of cottonwood trees. As if on signal, both guys turn and start grabbing and groping us. Used to wrestling with boys, I am the first one out of the car, and Marcie is right behind me.

Ed jumps in the front seat. Chuck yells, "You sluts think you're too good for us. You'll be sorry." He backs up his dad's big green Oldsmobile and peels out, leaving us standing in a thick cloud of dust.

Marcie looks at me. "How in the world are we going to get home?"

I sigh. "Nothing to do but start walking." We walk two or three miles and it's too hot to even talk. An older man pulls up beside us in an old Ford and asks, "You girls need a ride?"

It's Bud, a nice guy from Fort Pierre who has been fishing since early morning. We feel like he's safe as we know who he is and where he lives. We jump in his old Ford it smells like cigarette smoke and fish.

"How'd you get out here?"

"It's a long story," Marcie says.

Bud stops to let us out in front of the café. "Thank you so much," Marcie and I say, practically in unison.

"Anytime," Bud says as he pulls away.

The next week the scuttlebutt in school is about us having sex with the whole football team from the other school. Dorothy heard it from Jenny who heard it from Chuck who, coincidentally, is Jenny's boyfriend.

I feel as helpless and powerless as I do when my dad attacks me for no reason. How can we prove our innocence? We decide to say nothing. The gossip goes underground, but my feelings of resentment and anxiety don't. Mom's "What will people think?" rattles around in my brain.

I tell myself, *I don't care what people think. I don't care, I don't care, I don't care.*

But I do.

Chapter Thirteen
Chosen

I'm a junior in high school now and not working after school for Dan anymore. Hoping to have more time for fun, I take a job working at Floyd's on Friday and Saturday nights. It's a smaller café, with a different clientele—fewer hot constructions workers and more rancher-type good old boys. There I meet my friend Phillip Quin, a rich rancher who is drunk much of the time. Phillip treats me nice, always has something nice to say to me, and tips very well.

In the middle of September I rush in the store after school to see Mom. Mrs. Hagger sneers and says she had to "run home for something." All excited, I race the rest of the way home, crashing in the front door calling out, "Mom, Mom!" I'm floating on air and have tears shimmering in my eyes. "Mom!"

She comes out of the bedroom. "What?"

I'm so excited I can barely get the words out. "I've been nominated a queen candidate for the junior class!"

With a tone that only sounds mildly interested, she says, "Oh, that's nice. Here, zip me up. I have to go." She holds up her salt and pepper hair while I zip up the back of the dress she's just put on.

My overwhelming joy tumbles off cloud nine and crashes—thud—through the floor. I sink into the couch and watch her hustle out the front door. Trying to make excuses for her, I think, *She has no clue.* How could she know that all the boys were dismissed from the room while the girls voted on the king candidate. We choose Mike, a popular guy with dreamy green eyes who wears a big black cowboy hat. How could she know that all the girls were clustered in the hall outside the classroom door—except for me. I was idly looking out the window, waiting for the boys to vote. It wouldn't be me so why would I care who they pick? I half pay attention to the chatter of the girls.

"I bet they choose Mable."

"Or maybe it will be June."

I knew both Mable and June are gaga over Mike.

"For sure it will be whatever girl Mike likes."

All the girls are certain it will be one of those two, and June and Mable are each pretending to root for the other.

June is telling Mable, "I hope it's you."

Mable is saying, "Oh no, June, I'm sure Mike likes you better.

In fifteen minutes the door opens and somebody says, "You guys can come back in now."

How could Mom know that when we walk back in the classroom, the name Evelyn is right up there on the blackboard next to Mike's name?

I hear audible snorts and gasps of disbelief from the other girls, and I almost faint at the sight of my name. When the bell rings and the class files out I wait until everyone leaves and ask Mrs. Young, "Is this a joke?"

Mrs. Young gathers up her notebooks, smiles at me and says, "No, it's the real thing. Congratulations."

I wonder if Mom would understand if she'd ever take the time to listen to me?

In our school the class that sells the most tickets to the school carnival wins the king and queen contest. Everybody in the class is supposed to hustle. If any of the girls in my class sold even one ticket, I'm not aware of it. I am determined to win so I work my legs off running from business to business night after night selling tickets, going in and out of the bars even, asking everyone to buy tickets and telling them I'm the queen candidate.

"I have to have a formal and some new high heels, Mom." I break this news to her on a Saturday morning before she goes to work.

"I'll talk to Dad," she says on her way out the door. "Go see what you can find." Marcie and I go to Freda's on the hill by the St. Charles hotel. Freda is an eccentric little French woman who has great taste in clothes. We plow through racks of long dresses and find a glorious sky blue strapless, a vision in yards and yards of tulle that costs thirty dollars. It's perfect, and I ask Freda to save it for me. Then we go to Penny's to find shoes. A pair of silver two-inch heels are $2.95. I'll come back for them.

When I report back to Mom she gives me forty dollars and reminds me that "We work hard for our money."

On the final Wednesday before the carnival on Friday, I wait breathlessly for the count. It's close but our class comes in second. This is pretty good considering I pretty much did it all by myself.

The night of the big fall school carnival is my Cinderella's dream come true. I walk down the crepe-paper star-studded aisle on Mike's arm in my new blue tulle formal and silver shoes wondering *Is this for real? Am I really doing this?*

Mom, Dad and the boys are in the gym, sitting on the front bleachers with the other parents. "Yep," I overhear Dad say as I practically float by, "That's my daughter."

For a moment there we are just like a normal family.

§

Marcie's not dating Ted any more, not even sneaking around to meet him. "I love Ted," she says, "but he's too unreliable." What she really means is she dumped him for good because he hit her. She's now dating a rich guy, Bruce, from across the river. He's nice; I like him.

One day she asks me if I want to go on a blind date with Randy, a friend of Bruce's.

"Sure, that sounds like fun, What're we going to do?"

"Just go to the movies."

"What should I wear?"

"Just something nice, he always looks swell."

We have a great time at the movies. Randy *is* really nice. "Can I get you some popcorn and a coke?" he asks. We sit in the comfortable theater seats, spellbound by *The Creature From The Black Lagoon*. Randy casually drapes his arm over my shoulder. I feel pleasantly comfortable and drop my guard a little.

On the way home from the movie Randy asks, "Want to do this again next Saturday?"

Joy bubbles up in my throat almost choking my response. "Sure, that sounds like fun." He gives me a gentle peck on the cheek and says, "See you next Saturday."

The next Saturday Randy unexpectedly shows up at my house about one o'clock in the afternoon. I've been scrubbing the floor in an old pair of pedal pushers and my hair is a mess. I don't want Randy to see me like this.

"What are you doing here this early?"

"Come out here for a minute," he says, looking troubled.

I step out the front door to the sidewalk where he stands and nervously twists his cap in his hands.

"My dad says I can't date you, because you're not Catholic."

"Oh."

"I'm sorry. I like you."

Speechless I Turn fast and step up on the front porch. *Go back to your almighty fart—mouth Catholic dad. I sure don't need you . . . Thanks for nothing, God.*

For a moment there my hard shell had cracked a little, but now it's back double thick.

What is it with Catholics? Marcie tells me it is the only religion that counts; all the rest of us are going to hell.

Sometimes I worry about hell. Even when I go to church, which isn't often any more, all I ever hear is talk about sin. "Pride is a sin, envy is a sin, greed is a sin, vanity is a sin." I know I'm guilty of it all, so there's no hope for me.

Put it out of your mind. Don't think about it. You're already lost.

§

One balmy spring night Marcie and I walk down the street with our heads in the clouds singing the theme song from *Love is a Many Splendored Thing*. We are gaga over actor William Holden and actress Jennifer Jones and don't even notice the guys walking behind us. We've just seen the most romantic lovemaking scenes we've ever witnessed and are transported to dreamland by the scenes from the movie.

The guys walking behind us are making catcalls and whistles. I turn around to tell them off and see it's my brother Ted and his friend Harold. "You goofball," I toss out at Ted

"Yeah, you must be in dreamland. We've been following you since you left the movie, all the way down the hill." Ted smiles at Marcie. *He still cares for her.*

"This is my friend Harold. He's in the air force and just got home from boot camp."

Wow! Harold is spectacularly handsome, and I give him a smile. "Hi Harold" He is a compact, cocky guy with curly hair and a beautiful cleft chin. Mom has told me many times a cleft chin is a sign of strength.

Harold smiles back. "Hi."

Ted gets right to the point. "My friend Harold here is going to take you to the junior prom."

What? I don't even know him. "Ted, Mom says you are supposed to take me."

"Yeah, but Harold really wants to and I don't."

Harold nods his head in agreement. "Yes," he says, as he ducks his head sort of shyly. "I'd really like to do that. What kind of flowers do you like? What color is your dress?"

Really? A guy wants to know what kind of flowers I like?

I'm giddy. "I like roses and my dress is blue," I say, my smile growing.

"Oh, good it'll match my uniform." *He cares about a dress matching his uniform? Wow!*

The Friday night of the prom I have to go to the junior-senior banquet first where no dates are allowed. I arrange to meet Harold at Dan's Café. When I walk into Dan's wearing my blue frothy tulle formal, from the queen candidate days, Harold is waiting. My heart jumps like I've done a flying squirrel's landing, then jumps again. All decked out in his air force uniform, he hands me a white rose with a blue carnation wrist corsage decked out with a silver ribbon. *Oh, my gosh, he's so handsome. I'll love Ted forever for this.*

I feel like a princess as we walk the four blocks to the school gym where we enter the star-studded, spangled, crepe-paper fantasyland put together by the sophomores. We dance every dance and Harold's the best dancer I've ever danced with, including Bud from the bar. Tonight is a night dreams are made of.

After the prom all the kids I'm friends with go to a cabin on the island at the big lake. It's a beautiful spring night as the full moon sheds a light so brilliant it almost seems like daylight. We don't even need to turn headlights onto our picnic space.

Everybody is drinking and Harold asks, "Do you want a beer?"

I shake my head. "No, I don't drink."

"Then I won't either."

We sit on a log and talk for hours about everything. Harold takes off his uniform jacket and wraps it around my shoulders, saying, "I have to keep my girl warm."

Wow, my girl.

We get home just as the sun is peeking over the horizon. "Can I see you tonight?" he asks. "I'll meet you at the Legion hall for the dance."

I tell him yes, determined to go if it kills me. Harold is already there when I arrive. He's combed his curly hair in a DA (duck's ass) the popular Bobby Darin hairstyle so many of the other guys have. His pink shirttails flap when he dances as does the beer can opener hanging from one pierced ear. I've never seen a guy with a pierced ear before. Harold is so much fun. That night neither of us dances with anyone else.

We see each other almost every night and two nights before his furlough is up we have plans for a special Saturday night dress-up dinner. I'm to meet him at Dan's, but he doesn't show up. I sit there feeling deserted, angry, hurt, and confused. Dorothy and Myrna come in. "I thought you had a date."

I make a face. "So did I. Want to do something?"

Dorothy wags her head toward the door. "There's a dance at Blunt tonight."

"Yeah, but Blunt's twenty-five miles away."

Just then, Philip Quin, my rancher friend, walks in the front door of the café. "What you girls doin'?" he asks.

I'm struck with a brilliant idea. "Hey Phillip, we want to go to a dance at Blunt. Can we borrow your car?"

Phillip reaches in his pocket for the keys. "Sure, just don't wreck it."

The three of us pile in his car and head east for Blunt. The dance is already started, so I drive fast. When I realize I'm going down the road at a hundred miles an hour I force myself to slow down to eighty. We sing *The Yellow Rose of Texas* at the top of our lungs as we drive down the highway. We dance for a couple hours and deliver the car safely back to Phillip, finding him at the Silver Spur Bar.

Harold isn't around on Sunday. I don't hear from him on Monday. *I wonder if he's dead.*

"Ted have you seen Harold?" I ask, trying to sound like I don't care.

"He left yesterday for his new assignment in Casablanca."

I thought I knew you, Harold. I thought you cared for me. Why did you treat me like this?

Chapter Fourteen
Sinking

Dad is sitting at the kitchen table with his head in his hands when I get home from school for lunch. I tiptoe around him and put my finger to my lips when the other kids come in. When Mom comes in she goes to Dad and puts her hands on his shoulders. "It'll be all right, Lon. We'll get by. You'll get another job."

We kids eat in silence and leave for school as soon as possible. *Dad must have gotten fired.* That night I ask Mom, "What's wrong?" and she confirms my suspicion.

"Yes, Dad got fired."

It's strange having Dad home to make breakfast. He has the radio on full blast listening to Paul Harvey on WNAX. I even kind of like old Paul myself, but not the agriculture news, cattle prices, obituaries, or world news. I don't much care about the price of wheat or corn. I don't care what President Eisenhower is doing. I don't want breakfast either. It's all I can do to drag myself out of bed.

Dad's home looking like a whipped puppy every day, every night, and at noon when we come for lunch. I feel sorry for him until he takes it upon himself to monitor all my activities.

"You are disgrace to this family," he tells me. "Running day and night with that wild bunch of girls."

He doesn't know that I'm the ringleader of this "wild bunch of girls."

"Are you even going to school?"

I think I liked it better when he was never home.

Dad starts following me to school. He doesn't know I see him ducking behind a car or a building when I turn to look.

"Why is your dad following us?" Marcie asks.

I shake my head. I don't want it to be true, but now that's she's noticed, I have to come up with some explanation. "I guess because he's not going out and drinking anymore, he has nothing else to do."

I am completely embarrassed by Dad getting fired. It's never discussed at our house and I'm sure not going to say anything to Marcie, but this has to stop.

"By the way," Marcie says offhandedly, "when I drove mom to the airport last week at four-thirty in the morning, I saw your dad walking down the street with Melva. They had just come out of Melva's apartment."

My dad was walking down the street with the town whore at four thirty in the morning! I swallow the bile in my throat and say, "Oh yeah, they are friends. It doesn't mean anything."

She changes the subject just as we walk in the door at school.

When I get home after going first to Dan's Café and drinking a coke, then walking Marcie home, Dad's waiting for me.

"School gets out at four o'clock. Where have you been?"

"I stopped for a coke and I walked Marcie home."

"You're lying," he yells, "you got some pimply-faced guy out there you're shacking up with?"

Even if I do the right thing he calls it the wrong thing.

"You're wrong. Why are you following me to school anyway?"

"Because you're a liar and a cheat. I can't trust you. From now on I'm driving you to school and picking you up at four o'clock. Furthermore, you are grounded. You are going to graduate if it kills me."

The next morning, Dad's waiting in the car. Bill, Mike, and Bernie hustle off to school as usual, and Mom's still getting ready for work. *She's not going to stick up for me.* I open the door of the old green Studebaker. Dad sits behind the wheel smelling of tobacco and Aqua Velva, his straw hat at a jaunty angle as usual. I refuse to look in his direction and ride in silence the six blocks to school.

I knew Marcie would be waiting for me to walk with her. I hope she's not late to school. Marcie comes sliding into assembly just as the bell rings. "What happened to you?" she hisses.

"My dad's being a real pain in the ass." I shrug my shoulders in a helpless gesture that says I have no choice.

At noon I see his car right in front of the school. At four in the afternoon he's standing by the door waiting for me when I walk out. He motions in the direction of the car. "Get in," he commands.

"How long is Dad going to keep this up?" I ask my mom.

"Think of it this way, you've got your own chauffeur."

I try to giggle but it comes out more like a moan. "What's wrong with him, Mom?"

She points her finger at me. "He's your father. There is nothing wrong with him. You're lucky you even have a father."

She doesn't understand. She doesn't care. I blame her for his behavior. If she'd lay down the law, things would be a lot different around here.

I have to stay home, can't go to Dan's, and can't visit any of my friends. Nothing makes much sense. At supper nobody says anything about it. I wonder what my brothers are thinking.

Ted leaves for work before I get up for school and gets home after I do. I don't know if he even knows what's going on.

Dad is nice to my friends when they come knocking on the door and even invites them to stay for supper a couple of times, but they politely decline. Marcie, Dorothy, Shelia, and sometimes Myrna sit on the bank of the river with me behind our house, talking and smoking cigarettes. Sheila says "You sure have a nice dad." Sheila's dad abandoned her years ago. *Maybe she's right.*

I pretend to like the game for a couple of weeks, hiding my humiliation from my friends and the other kids at school. I try to draw as little attention to myself as possible. Dad always says, "It's nobody's business what goes on in our house." Mom always says, "Never let your right hand know what your left hand is doing." So I smile at Dad when others can see and ignore him when there's no one around. I "rise above it"—Mom's rule for dealing with anything unpleasant.

It's a Saturday at the end of April when I see Dad packing up the old pickup with tools and clothes. *I wonder what he's doing? I wonder if he's missed his wine and whiskey yet?* Mike and I found some bottles of wine and a fifth of whiskey under the seat and threw them in the river.

Dad and I haven't really spoken to each other for days. I comb my hair and hike down to the store where Mom's working. "Where's Dad going?"

She glances up from the papers she's filling out at the counter. "He's decided to go work on our farm for the summer. Get back home and get your work done. Let's have fried chicken for supper, and boil some potatoes—make them soupy the way Dad likes them."

She's forgotten I have to go to work at four o'clock. *How could she forget? I do it every Friday and Saturday.*

"Okay," I say, knowing Dad will fix supper and grateful I won't be there. I walk to the other side of the store, buy a package of Pall Mall cigarettes, and head for home.

§

Dan asks me to come to work at the café for the summer. I get to work forty, sometimes even forty-eight hours a week, and I love what I do. Esther, Donna, and I usually work together. This is something I'm good at. Here people say please and thank you and Dan says, "Good work, Evelyn," something I never hear at home.

With these kind of hours, I seldom see Marcie. She's with Bruce anyway and they spend all their time at the lake swimming and hanging out. On the days I work nights I go there too. Often Ted and his buddies are there.

I don't know how to swim and share Dad's incredible fear of water. Everybody in our family knows Dad is terrified of water. If he dreams about water he says it means something really bad is going to happen and he's usually right. Seven big sows died in our farmyard one hot August afternoon when I was young and Dad said he'd dreamed about water the night before.

It's the dog days of summer—a time when superstitious people think going in the water will make you sick. Myrna's mom won't let her go swimming during dog days, so Dorothy and I go alone this Wednesday afternoon.

The beach is full of kids. Allen and his friend Rod are here. I think Rod is dreamy. He comes to our house a lot but rarely gives me a glance, except for a quick "Hi." I wonder if Allen told him to leave me alone.

I see Allen and Rod in the water not too far out so I wade in and head for them. Almost there, I call out, "Hey Ted. Hey guys." Right then I step in a hole and I'm immediately engulfed in water. It goes in my mouth and up my nose. I go down and then my head pops up, then I go under again. I feel like I'm in a watery grave.

Then Rod gets to me and pulls me up. Fighting for my life, I punch him. My body is flailing like a dead chicken's does when it's just lost its head.

Rod yells, "Stop fighting me!"

I try to stop, but it's impossible. Rod drags me to shore still fighting like a banshee, while everyone watches. He throws me on the sand where I cough and sputter but I'm breathing.

Ted asks me, "Are you okay?" Then turning to Rod he says, "Thanks man, she coulda drowned."

Rod is rubbing his face. "She's got a mean right hook."

The rest of the day, I lie in the sun thinking *I almost drowned—I almost drowned—I almost drowned.* What would my mother say? The laughter and voices of the other kids are strangely distant, when I hear these distinct words: "Thank God you are alive."

I look around. Nobody is paying the slightest bit of attention to me. *Who could have said that?* Actually, it sounded like my mother's voice. *Nah.*

§

"Have you seen what's happening at the Sinclair station?" Myrna and Dorothy are sitting in the back booth at Dan's.

"No, what's happening?"

Myrna's excited. "We walked over there and the station is being refurbished and the café in back of it has people in it and it's just about ready to open. Maybe I'll apply for a job there."

Dorothy thinks this a good idea. "Me too," she says.

I gotta go check this out. By the time I get a chance to go there, Dorothy has a job already and all the scoop. An older couple is running it. They have a daughter, Susie, who is fifteen and heavy-set and acts sort of babyish. They also have three really good-looking boys, men actually, who have gotten jobs on the dam.

I meet the guys when they come into Dan's one Saturday night: Herman, Gary, and Joe. *Dorothy's right—they are hunky, handsome beasts, especially Gary.* In no time these guys become a part of our crowd. Myrna really likes Joe.

§

I'm ready for my senior year to start. Summers aren't as much fun just working a full-time job.

Dad's spending more time at home since he found a new job as a security guard at the capitol building. He tells Mom, "High school kids run in and out of there like they own the place. Can you believe it? Well, not on my watch. From now on I'm locking all the doors and only adults can come in and only if they sign in."

I'm sure glad Dad wasn't there when we were running around in there. I have wonderful memories of that place.

Ted has decided to join the military, prompted by aimlessness, a promise of more money, and a couple of friends in the service. He breaks it to Mom and Dad at Sunday dinner. "I'm getting sworn in to the air force tomorrow."

Dad says, "Might as well. Then we'll know where you are." Dad rarely knows where Ted is.

Mom sort of gasps, then tells him, "Good for you. Everybody has to do their part for our country. I'm proud of you."

The next morning Ted leaves for the bus depot to go to Sioux Falls to be sworn in.

"Don't let Evelyn drive my car," he instructs Mom and Dad as he hugs Mom good-bye at the front door. His silver two-door 1950 Buick Roadmaster is his pride and joy. Even though the rusty junk heap is banged up from having been wrecked by a previous owner, he owns it and paid for it with his own money.

When Ted leaves so does my security blanket. It's like a part of me got on the bus with him. The minute the front door closes behind him I feel the full force of it. I feel empty, lost, stripped of my protection. Abandoned, bereft, orphaned.

Even though we don't spend all our time together, he'd never been far away. Even when he came home drunk in the middle of the night, even when he ran away, even when I was at someone else's house, he was my anchor. I knew if I did anything wrong, I would have to answer to Ted. But now he's left for boot camp and he can't come home even if he wants to. I'm lost without him.

The hollow space in my gut calls for something, but what? I've never touched alcohol and only smoked when Ted couldn't see me. Now who is there to care?

§

A salesman is sitting in our living room talking to Mom when I come in from my shift at the café one August evening. He has some books and papers spread out and is showing them to her. Dorothy's mother gave him my name thinking I might be interested in learning shorthand at night school. She thought Dorothy might go for it, but she wants to marry Cleve and be a housewife.

"Can you see me in an office?" Dorothy asks me.

"Nope, you're the last person I would expect to work in an office." She nods emphatically when I tell her this.

The man in our living room is impressing Mom. He's young, sort of good looking, his suit and tie fit perfectly, and he smells good. "Oh, yes," he tells Mom. "If she," pointing now at me, "learns how to do shorthand she can be making big money in as little as three months. There's a huge demand for secretaries and court reporters. They make as much as three dollars an hour. A good stenographer can have her pick of jobs."

I make fifty cents an hour as a waitress so I'm intrigued. Besides, it sounds so easy.

Mom looks at me. "Are you interested in this?"

Mr. Suit-and-Tie presses his point. "I have a special going on right now. I can sign her up for just four hundred dollars. She'll make that easy the first month and you can pay twenty-five dollars a month until she can handle the rest of it herself." He practically oozes enthusiasm. He says, "Our next class starts in September," then pushes the papers and a pen toward Mom.

I feel like Mom wants me to do this when she asks me, "Do you want to do this?"

I look from the salesman to her and answer, "I guess."

Dad throws a fit! And then another fit! "Edith, how could you let her do this?" He stomps around the kitchen, goes out the front door, slams it, then comes back in slamming the door again. "What is wrong with both of you? Edith, how could you?" Without waiting for an answer, he stalks back to the front door and goes out and slams the door again.

"He'll be okay," Mom tells me. "He just needs to get used to the idea." Then Mom says something I think is really strange. "Someday you will realize that God has reasons for everything he does. This is why I never try to tell people what to do."

Are you kidding me?

Now that shorthand school is a done deal, I'm sort of excited. The lure of big money pulls at me. I see myself behind a desk wearing a beautiful suit and jotting down notes for some rich business man, maybe even a lawyer.

Marcie is really mad when I tell her I'm not going back to school this fall. "But that's terrible. Who will I walk to school with? Why would you do this?"

Feeling defensive, I counter, "I hardly ever see you anymore anyway now that you're engaged. You do everything with Bruce."

She's furious. "You'll be sorry."

§

There's a feeling of promise in the crisp, sun-dappled fall morning. I'm home alone with my thoughts rampaging through my head. From my front porch I can see everyone else walking to school laughing and bantering in their fresh new skirts and sweaters, brand new bookbags over their shoulders.

It's okay, I tell myself, *you didn't fit in all that well anyway.* But I feel lost and alone and betrayed by my mother. I know I'm the one who said yes. *Why do I feel so empty, cold, and lonely? I don't care.*

§

In just a few weeks Mike announces he's quitting school to go to work for a rancher in the area. This makes me sad as he's a genius. He and I used to be so close and now I can't even talk to him.

"What happened to your dream of being a scientist?"

He shrugs as if the question is not worth his time. "I got a job."

Mike has gone from being a sweet, lovable goofball with a big heart to an angry jackass with a foul mouth.

I just know something is eating him alive, but what? We have always been allies but now he calls me names, and kicks at chairs.

He sits at the dining room table and demands service. "Where's my coffee?" he yells.

"Get it yourself. Stop yelling at me."

He gets up and punches a hole in the wall. "I am not the maid," he says.

"Well, I'm not the maid either, you nincompoop."

"Yeah, you're just a parasite."

Something unspeakable has happened to him, I just know it. My heart breaks for the fourteen-year-old innocent boy who is going through something I know nothing about.

When I try to talk to Mom about his behavior, she tells me, "He's being a boy. This is how boys are."

Dan only needed me for the summer, so I march down to the Eat In, the new café at the Sinclair station. "Yes," they tell me, "Now that Susie is going back to school we can use a daytime waitress."

Marie, Susie's mom, opens the place at seven. I walk in at nine o'clock so she can leave or work in the kitchen or do whatever she has to do. I like it there. I see a lot of Herman, Gary, and Joe. They tease me.

Gary has a crush on Sheila's beautiful sister Trixie, but at the moment, Trixie is in love with Ted.

Trixie and Sheila's mom is a tough little woman who is rarely home as she works all the time at two jobs. Trixie is a glamorous, gorgeous, nineteen-year-old blond who looks terrific in tight sweaters and blue jeans. She plays a guitar and dates a striking, lanky, drop-dead handsome cowboy from the nearby Indian reservation. He is fun, personable, and plays his own guitar. He writes songs about Trixie's beautiful blue eyes and sings them to her lovingly. The small trailer house belonging to Sheila's mother rocks with music when Trixie is in it but she has her own apartment across the river.

Shelia and I relax on the floor listening to them play and sing as often as possible. Their love for each other ignites all my romantic fantasies. When I watch them together the longing I feel to be loved is like a burning hunger.

§

It's seven p.m. on September 15, and I'm sitting behind a long table in a cold, ugly room in an old brick warehouse. The plaster in the classroom is cracked and the one bare lightbulb hanging down in the center makes the room look spooky. The old-maid-type teacher hands out books and shorthand tablets to seven of us. She marks us all present then starts speaking gobbledygook. Little squiggles here, little dots there, a curling figure and a loop—it all means something.

I try to pay attention but it's all Greek to me and very, very boring. The first week two girls drop out. I start missing more classes than I'm attending. This is the building Trixie's apartment is in, so I go upstairs and hang out with her. I'm not built for shorthand. It makes no sense to me. In three weeks I drop out and start working full time at the Eat In.

In two weeks word reaches me that Susie told some girls in school that I stole money from their cash register. I'm waiting at Dan's Café for her when school ends for the day. When she comes in, I confront her.

Almost immediately Dan comes over. "Take it outside girls," he commands.

Out to the sidewalk we go followed by about fifteen high-school kids. "Susie, why would you say a stupid thing like that? I thought we were friends."

All two hundred and fifty pounds of Susie bristles. "Well, there was ten dollars missing from the register. Can you prove you didn't take it?" I leap on her big body and she falls to the ground, her skirt riding up around her waist. I'm pounding her head into the sidewalk when somebody yells, "Stop." It's my brother Mike. He walks over and pulls Susie's dress down.

I say, "Tell these people what you said is not true. Tell them!"

In a weak voice Susie says, "It's not true. I made it up."

At supper Dad says, "I talked to old Ed this afternoon. He said 'Boy, Lon, that's some kid you got there. A real scrapper.' I was really proud until I found out he was talking about my daughter."

I look up at his face and I can tell he's still really proud.

§

One Sunday I use Ted's car to pick up a bunch of girls. We chase up and down the highway, cruise up and down Main Street, and drive out to the cemetery. Some guys follow us out and we stop to talk to them for a while.

The door to the car was hanging open and when I try to drive away it catches on the bumper of the guys car. It's now dented and hanging crooked. When I roll to a stop in front of my house, I'm terrified. *What's Dad going to say?* Weak with fear, I wait for him to discover the damage. Sure enough when he walks in the first thing he says is, "What happened to the car?"

"What do you mean?"

"The door's all banged up."

"Yeah, somebody ran into me."

"Are you sure you didn't try to yank the door off?"

"You never believe anything I say." I glare at him belligerently.

He's really ranting now. "Well, it's going to cost at least three hundred dollars to fix it. You darn kids, are always breaking and wrecking stuff. I can't have anything decent around here."

You can't? That's Ted's car and he's going to kill me.

I shrug my shoulders figuring it's best to say nothing and just let him rant.

"Give me the keys. You are not driving this car again."

Okay, no car, no shorthand class. I don't know if anybody even notices I'm not going.

The next time Trixie comes home to Sheila's house, I ask her, "If I can find a full-time job in Pierre, can I move in with you? I'll pay half the rent."

She thinks for a few minutes then says, "Okay, but it will cost you thirty dollars a month."

§

When Ted comes home from boot camp a few weeks later, he finds the door hanging off his car and he is not happy. "I told you not to let Evelyn drive it," he yells at Mom and Dad. "I told you what would happen."

This sort of puts a damper on his reunion with us, but I'm thrilled to see him and Mom can't do enough for him.

Ted's home for thirty days. During this time, he runs around renewing acquaintances with his friends, partying at night, and when he's not sleeping in, working at the Standard gas station.

On the nights he comes in so drunk he can hardly walk. I take some money from his billfold. He doesn't remember how much he spends the night before when he's drinking. After all, I clean up his messes, cook his food, do his laundry, iron his shirts, and put creases in his jeans.

I'm mad at him because we don't do anything together. My former partner in crime is right in front of me and he won't speak to me because he's mad about his car.

This time when he leaves, he takes his car back to California with him. I tell myself, *I'm glad he's gone,* but the truth is I feel like he died.

Chapter Fifteen
Giving In

It's a crisp cool, almost-Halloween night—one of those perfect, pleasant, windless nights with a full moon. A bunch of us leave the Saturday night dance early as the music is not that great. The cab of Herman's old green truck is full of people so eight of us climb up on the running board, throw our legs over the wooden sides, and climb in the back. We're wrapped up in coats and blankets to keep warm.

I don't know where the bottle of sloe gin comes from. It's passed around a couple of times before my resistance melts like butter in an oven and the thick red liquid goes down like gloppy syrup.

I can't believe I'm doing this. I promised I never would. Oh shut up, everyone else is doing it.

Tipping the bottle up to my mouth, I feel daring, giddy, and divided. I quickly push down the wavering guilt and take another big swig, and wipe my mouth with the back of my hand.

Nothing happens. Why would anyone drink this?

The bottle comes around again and I take another gulp. Then it hits—a slow, warm, heat washes over me. My lips feel sort of numb, but the rest of me is blissful. The absence of emotional pain is ecstasy. I can't wait for another swallow.

So this is how it feels.

For the first time in my life I don't feel dumb, stupid, or afraid.

The next day I avoid going to church because my head feels as big as a basketball and it hurts to move it. *Why go anyway? Church is just a big lie, a way to keep stupid people in line.*

Drinking gives me temporary relief. I never knew what I was missing. Now I do it as often as the opportunity presents itself.

The day after I always loathe myself and rack my brain in a struggle to remember what I said or did. I know I fought for my virginity on more than one occasion, yelling for help from my friends when someone tries to pull my pants off in a darkened car parked at the gravel pit, or in a field somewhere. Fortunately, there is always a group of us.

I don't like the taste of sloe gin. I can't stand beer, and whiskey stinks, but wow the temporary feeling of bliss and power it spreads through me . . . I feel beautiful, accomplished, as if I can be anything, do anything—and it's worth the suffering the next day.

Sober I always feel two feet lower than the sidewalk. I hide even from myself by following Mom's famous edicts:

"Ignore it and it will go away."

"Don't let anyone know you care."

"Rise above it."

"Never let your right hand know what your left is doing."

"Don't wear your heart on your sleeve."

"Don't cry; crying makes you ugly."

It never once, not even once, occurs to me this might be the same reason Dad drinks.

When I drink, I cry to love songs and I drunkenly blabber my sob story to unsuspecting friends. This turns people off so much they tell Dorothy to tell me I can't hang out with them anymore if I don't stop it.

It takes a supreme effort to shut off all of my emotions when I'm drinking but I'm determined to be the life of the party, the girl who doesn't give a hoot, the clown who dances on the table. I'm also going back to being the girl who if you look at me crossways, I'll deck you and spit in your face.

§

Sheila, in the meantime, is falling in love with Lee, a pint-sized, muscle-bound, hard-drinking, hard-fighting hunk of hooligan, who happens to be Esther's other brother. They want to get married, but Sheila's mom says, "No. Sixteen is too young."

Sheila is brokenhearted when Lee moves on. She cries on my shoulder for a while, but replaces Lee with Jude who is from an Indian reservation north of us in another state. Everybody likes Jude who is here to work on the dam. He is intriguing, darkly handsome, sweet, kind, and beyond interesting. He tells us ghost stories about spirits and Big Foot. In a dim room in Sheila's mom's trailer house, we circle around Jude on the floor while he weaves his tales.

"I've actually met up with the devil," he claims. He weaves his tales with skill, sucking us all into his magic web.

I wonder, *How much truth is there to his spirit stories?* But he's really convincing.

Sheila doesn't say a word to me about her plans. She and Jude just run off to the reservation and get married. When they come back, they move into their own trailer house in a trailer court down by the river.

§

I'm walking around Pierre putting in job applications when Mr. Styles, the manager of the Ben Franklin, offers me a job as a cashier. "Be here Monday morning at eight-thirty. Wear whatever you want, except jeans. We're open six days a week, closed on Sunday. When Christmas comes, we'll be open until nine in the evening. On the days you work until nine you won't have to come in until noon. If you work out, you'll get a raise after Christmas. Any questions?"

Yes, what do you pay? I'm too chicken to ask, so I just wait and see.

"No sir, I will see you Monday."

I'm elated. "Mom, I got a job at Ben Franklin. Trixie says I can live in her apartment with her so I can walk to work."

She looks at me and says, "I hope you know what you're doing."

Sheila picks me up Sunday afternoon. Filled with anticipation, I lug my suitcase up the two flights of stairs and move in with Trixie. It's official, I'm on my own.

The Ben Franklin is full of intriguing smells. The candy counter is right in front with its fresh popped popcorn, just-formed fudge, and divinity filled with walnuts. Lining the aisles are kitchen gadgets, sewing supplies, perfumes, hair dyes, and lots of clothes and toys.

Counting out change at the cash register is exhilarating. *Maybe I'm good at this. Maybe they'll like me here.* I look like an adult but I feel like a fake.

Two weeks of pretending to be an adult later, I'm handed my first paycheck on my way out the door. I can't wait to see what it is. Ducking into the shop next door I rip open the envelope.

I am getting a dollar an hour wage. It's my turn to buy groceries and Trixie needs fifteen dollars for half a month's rent, so I won't have much left. Oh well.

§

It's the night before Thanksgiving. Trixie has changed from being in love with Ted to being in love with Gary. Gary and Herman bring beer—three six-packs. We laugh, cook, talk, and dance to the radio.

What the heck, I don't have to go to work tomorrow. I'll go home in the morning.

Drunk! We're all drunk. Gary and Herman leave, not sure when—sometime after I fall into bed, too goobered up to keep up with them.

Thanksgiving morning Trixie drops me at my house. I walk in the door to the smell of turkey roasting about ten with bloodshot eyes and a raging headache.

Mom is in the kitchen and obviously not happy with me. "Where have you been? I thought you'd be here last night."

"What's the big deal? I'm here now."

"We had to call an ambulance for your father at four this morning. You should have been here."

I'm a terrible daughter. I should have been here. Guilt hits me like a well-aimed bullet.

Dad had a gall-bladder attack and needs surgery. Our family sits in his hospital room, cracking jokes, talking about the news, watching Dad smoke Camels and eats Jello.

"I'm not having surgery." Dad has made up his mind. "I'm not paying six hundred dollars so some doctor can line his pockets."

In two days Dad's back at his job.

§

The dime store is packed with people, and signs of Christmas are everywhere—the music, the tinsel, the sparkling array of decorations, and the special gifts. The sounds of *Silent Night* or *Jingle Bells* blare inside and out and can be heard two blocks away.

When the manager compliments me for being "efficient and polite," it makes me work even harder.

"I don't think we're going to have much of a Christmas this year," Mom confides on one of my Sunday afternoon visits. "Taxes on the house and farm ate up all our money. I can barely make ends meet."

"It's okay, Mom. I have a job." *Hmm—if I buy all the presents for the boys, then she can buy my watch.* "How about if I buy the presents from Santa for the boys, then you won't have to worry about it?"

She looks relieved. "That is really nice of you."

Picking out gifts for the boys is fun. I put shirts, gun-and-holster sets, corduroy pants, pajamas, puzzles, pick-up sticks, Tinker Toys, and Lifesaver books (looks like a book but is filled with candies) on layaway. I hold my head up higher than normal as I take on this grown-up responsibility.

The next day I walk across the street to Feinstein's, the only upscale store in town, and try on a winter coat for mom. *If it fits me, it'll fit her.* The one she wears is five years old. The coat is e-l-e-g-a-n-t, a princess-style swagger coat, ankle length, purple- and gray-checked wool, double breasted with four leather buttons and a stand-up collar. It costs two weeks' pay. I put thirty dollars down on it and ask for Mrs. Williams to hold it for me.

"My mom's going to love this coat. It's so stylish," I tell Peggy, my co-cashier.

When Mom stops in the store one evening, Peggy tells her, "I hope if I ever have a daughter she loves me as much as your daughter loves you."

Mom looks at Peggy like she's daft.

Peggy has listened to me blather on about how much my mother loves Christmas, how she bakes ten different kinds of cookies, makes mincemeat, apple, and pumpkin pies, whips up fudge, and red and green popcorn balls." She knows all about how our Christmas Eve is always a big-big deal with oyster stew, chili, homemade ice cream, church at ten, and hanging up the stockings.

"You still do that?" Peggy asks me in disbelief.

"Yep, we all do it. It's a tradition."

I'm sort of smug about our traditions. I don't tell her that when Dad brings in the ice to pack around the wooden ice-cream maker on Christmas Eve, it's obvious he's had too many Tom and Jerry cocktails. But who cares? He's home.

I buy some Prince Albert tobacco for Dad for his pipe, also some Aqua Velva shaving lotion as I love the way this smells on him. I want my parents to know I love them. After all, if somebody gives you a gift, picked out just for you, something they know you will really like—that's love . . . right?

The break room at work is filled with homemade candy, cookies, and fruitcake. We all run back there to nibble the sweet stuff on our breaks. Everybody's talking about the big store party planned for the week between Christmas and New Year's, after the work dies down. The invitation on the break room bulletin board says six o'clock at the country club, choice of a beef filet or chicken divan, dancing, and gift exchange. I'm really looking forward to this party as I've never been to the country club.

Dorothy stops in the store with her arms full of packages and lingers until I'm through waiting on a customer, then invites me to a Christmas party at Marso's on Friday night. She holds out her hand and says, "See my Christmas present?" It's a small diamond ring set in a gold band. Not spectacular, but nice. I don't have time to ooh and ah so I just say, "Congratulations!"

I can't get away from work fast enough Friday night. I wear my new black velvet dress to work so I'll be ready to party. A lot of beer has gone down a lot of throats by the time I walk in the door. I know everyone there with the exception of Cleve's parents. His dad, a short, round man in bib overalls and checkered shirt, is having a high old time.

Giving In

A beer floats into my hands. Then another. I try a Tom and Jerry. *Yuck, not for me.* Somebody gives me a shot of whiskey. "Bottoms up," he says. We dance to Jo Stafford, Elvis Presley, the Four Aces belting out *Tell Me Why*, and Doris Day tunes on the blaring jukebox. My lips are numb. I feel no pain. I don't even know who I'm dancing with. I want to be with Gary, but Trixie is with Gary so I can only stare at them enviously.

I wake up wondering, *How did I get home?* I search my brain and come up with a vague memory of Gary putting me in the car.

"Did I make a fool of myself last night?" I ask Trixie.

"Not any worse than usual."

What does that mean?

"Oh my gosh, I have to get to work." I grab some clothes, put some pancake makeup over my blotchy face, run a brush through my hair and hike down the hill. The Ben Franklin door is open and I'm a half an hour late.

Peggy won't look at me. Just outside the break room I hear her tell our boss, "Phew, I could get drunk just standing next to her."

I must reek like stale beer.

The manager comes up to front of the store where I'm trying hard to concentrate on cashiering. "Have a good time last night?"

Do I really smell that bad?

Only five more days until Christmas Eve. It's a party every night this week with a hangover every morning. My paycheck on Friday is enough to get the things I have on layaway for the boys, plus twenty dollars extra. I march across the street and pick up Mom's coat. Mrs. Williams has wrapped it beautifully and says I can pay the remaining thirty dollars after Christmas.

It's Christmas Eve day. I haul my Christmas treasures up to Trixie's. She's not here but Gary is sprawled on the couch. "Will you give me a ride home?" I holler from the bedroom where I've thrown my gifts on the bed and I'm stuffing clothes in a bag.

"Yes, and pack up the rest of your stuff too, because Trixie doesn't want you here anymore. She doesn't have the nerve to tell you, but I do."

Dazed, I sit on the bed. I was going to find something to eat but now I've lost my appetite. When Trixie comes in, she smiles half apologetically and hands me a beer.

Back at home, I lug my carefully planned treasures in the house and put them in my bedroom. Later I help Mom play Santa and we put all the boys' gifts in and under their stockings. To my surprise, Mom has a lot of gifts for them also.

I thought she couldn't afford gifts this year! I put Mom's beautifully wrapped coat under the tree. When I get to bed, I dream about what my watch will look like and I can hardly sleep. *Will it be gold or silver? Will it have an expansion band or a leather one?*

When the boys get up at the crack of dawn I am as excited as they are. I watch them hoot and holler over their holster sets, their Tinker Toys, their games and puzzles. When I reach for my own stocking I find the usual orange, a candy cane, and some chocolate. *No watch!* I open the gifts under the stocking—some stationery, a book, a new blouse. *No watch. Maybe it's under the tree.*

The packages under the tree are frantically freed from their beautiful wrappings and ribbons. I feel proud as Mom turns all around, modeling her new coat. "This is too much. You shouldn't have."

In one package for me there is a baby-blue nylon turtleneck sweater with a matching wool skirt. I try to gush over it but only manage to say, "This is great. Thanks a lot."

As soon as possible I escape to my room feeling sick to my stomach. I feel crushed. I try to tell myself a watch is not that important. I could have just bought one for myself instead of spending all my money on everybody else.

It doesn't matter. I'm just a spoiled brat. I think I have to have everything. Other people are important too. At least the little boys are happy, isn't that enough? But why doesn't Mom love me?

Mom comes to the door of my room to tell me to hurry up and get ready to go to Aunt Helen's for dinner. It's sixty miles to Seneca and she doesn't want to be late.

She acts surprised when she sees I'm upset. "What's wrong?"

"I thought I was going to get a watch for Christmas."

"I told you I didn't have any money. Here, I'll let you wear mine."

I shake my head. "No, I don't want to wear yours. Don't pay any attention to me, I'm just a spoiled brat." I swallow my feelings of betrayal and disappointment and wear my new skirt and sweater to Aunt Helen's for Christmas dinner.

Rise above it. Ignore it. Tune it out. Next time buy your own watch.

Walking in the door at work Tuesday, I sense there's something going on when Peggy doesn't even ask how my Christmas was. Mr. Styles stops me near the coat rack and he's not smiling. "We enjoyed having you here over Christmas, but Peggy can handle it now." The look on his face tells me he is lying.

No country club Christmas party for me. I feel as if all eyes are on me while I'm gathering my stuff from my locker in the back room. Plastering on a smile I walk out with my head high. Nobody looks in my direction. Nobody says a word.

Don't wear your heart on your sleeve. Never let them see you care.

§

Dorothy and Cleve were married by the justice of the peace just before Christmas. I'm feeling insulted because they didn't tell anyone beforehand. Their honeymoon was a trip to see Cleve's sister in North Dakota.

The newlyweds and Sheila go with me to Marso's Bar on New Year's Eve. I guzzle a coke, no alcohol for me ever again.

Sheila and I dance with a group of good-looking college guys home on break. One asks me to go sit in his car with him. I'm flattered but I'm swearing off men too. I say, "Why on earth would I want to sit in a car with a dim-witted idiot home from college?" He looks shattered but I don't care. I feel justified.

New Year's Day 1955 is uneventful. Our family dinner, Dad's famous beef stew, is accompanied by all the leftover baked goods mom slaved over before Christmas. The boys are building things with their new Tinker Toys. Mike and I play cards with Mom and Dad.

Ted is home for a few days. Once when I woke up at noon still drunk from an all-night party, I hear him telling Mom, "She's the most selfish, self-centered brat you guys have. She never thinks about anybody but herself."

Is he right, am I a selfish self-centered brat? Or is he just mad because I didn't iron his jeans?

Chapter Sixteen
Back Home

No one questions my moving back home. I'm okay with their assumption that my job was only going to last through Christmas. It feels good to be in my own room, sleeping in my own bed. Mike's got a job and has gone off somewhere. Everybody is back to life as "normal."

I wander aimlessly around the house when it occurs to me I can't breathe very well. My chest hurts. My nose is running. I'm hot and cold at the same time. When Mom comes home for lunch, I tell her.

"Take some aspirin, drink some hot tea, and go to bed." I stay in bed immersing myself in Reader's Digest books for a couple of days, before I ask Sheila to drive me to the doctor.

"Pneumonia," the doctor says. "You need to be admitted to the hospital." The nurses rush around, give me a hospital gown, take my temperature, and a blood sample, hand me a handful of pills, and give me a shot in my butt.

I call Mom at the store before I sink into a deep sleep. Mom, Dad, and the boys come in my room just after seven o'clock. "The doctor tells me you'll be here for a week," Mom says. "Why didn't you tell me you felt this bad?"

I was just trying to do what you taught me—ignore it and it will go away, and if you can't ignore it, rise above it.

Dorothy comes to visit me in the hospital." Cleve needs a job and he knows he can work in the creamery in Rapid City. I am going to look for a job as a waitress there. Why don't you come with us?" The day after I am released from the hospital, I pack my suitcase and leave while Mom and Dad are at work.

After two days in Rapid City I have a job as a waitress in Leonard's Café downtown where I'll work eleven to seven.

Cleve has found us a basement apartment. The rooms are dark, musty caves and everything smells like mold. The tiny bathroom, with the stool, sink, and bathtub practically on top of each other, is a nightmare. I sleep on a broken-down gray couch, and keep my clothes in the hall closet.

It is hard being here with a married couple. Not only do they have each other, while I have no one, I can't help but hear their sexual activities night after night. Cleve works long hours. Dorothy's working evenings at a supper club so we rarely talk to each other.

When it comes time to pay the twenty-five dollars that is my half of the rent for the second month, Cleve tells me nicely, "This just isn't working out. You need to go find your own place, Evelyn. Dorothy feels torn between me and you. She can't enjoy making love with you in the next room on the couch."

I give him a hug. "I understand. Will you drive me to the bus depot? I think I'll go home." I appreciate Cleve just telling it like it is, with no pretense or guessing games. I'm not mad or hurt, and even feel relieved. Being here wasn't what I had hoped for and I'm excited to be going home.

Leonard isn't happy when I stop to tell him I'm leaving the next morning at six on the way to the bus depot. The big red jackrabbit bus is only half full so I'm glad I can spread out. Snow is piled up on the sides of the highway and the bright sun out the window lies about how cold it really is. On the four-hour ride home we stop in every little town.

Mom and Dad don't act surprised to see me when I come walking back in, suitcase in hand. *Oh, were you gone?* their attitude seems to be saying. But Mom makes me my favorite lemon meringue pie after supper and Dad throws no verbal barbs at me.

I wonder if they are happy or are they mad? At least the little boys are happy to see me. Ted will be home on leave again soon and I'm suddenly desperate to see him again. He's been giving me the silent treatment and won't answer my letters.

I have no trouble connecting with my old crowd—Sheila, Dorothy, Cookie, Dixie, Myrna They're all at their new hangout, Lafa's Café, Sunday afternoon when I walk in to welcoming squeals and hugs.

On Monday after school I catch up with Marcie. I really missed her. We have a coke at Dan's but we are no longer on the same playing field. She's planning her wedding to Bruce and is full of herself. "I wish I could have you in my wedding, but you're not Catholic, so all you can do is come watch us."

There it is again. Catholics have a bizarre attitude toward those of us who apparently are going to hell because we're Protestants.

"Don't we all worship the same God?" I ask her. Not that I even believe in God anymore, but it sounds good. Actually, this is not true. I believe there is a God, I just believe with all my heart that he doesn't know there is a me.

Marcie smiles at me. "I don't make the rules." The coke tastes flat and my stomach sinks to my shoes. "See ya later," I tell her as we go our separate ways.

I need a job. Dan's not hiring. A new club is opening on the edge of town, just a mile past the Statesman—the supper club where some of my friends are working. An ad in the newspaper says: "Wanted: experienced waitress for new exclusive private nightclub. Night hours, no Sundays. Call for more information."

When I call the number Dave Smith answers. I give him the low-down on my experience. He's dismayed to find out I'm only seventeen, because I'm "just what he's looking for." He waffles. "You have to be eighteen to serve alcohol, but maybe we can work around this. Come out at three on Thursday and we'll talk."

The long, low brick building with no windows is dark and mysterious and smells of varnish, wax, and the new leather of the booths. Gilded mirrors hang above a carved mahogany bar. A huge dance floor has flashing red, yellow, and green lights and a state-of-the-art jukebox with all the latest music. Velvet curtains cover parts of the windowless walls and silver brocaded wallpaper in slivers creates flashing stripes on the wall. The soft red leather booths run along one wall and a gleaming back granite floor completes the picture.

Dave takes my name, telephone number, and asks me few questions. "When can you start?" he wants to know.

"I have to ask my Mom. I don't have transportation."

He has the answer. "I'll come to your house and pick you up and I'll bring you home when the club closes."

Mom's not sure about this when I tell her what I'm up too. "A bar? I don't think this is good idea. Can't you do something else?"

If there was something else, I'd be doing it. It's February and no one is hiring. I simply say, "No."

When Dave calls to find out if I can take the job, I let him talk to Mom on the telephone. He tells her I can just serve the food and he will serve all the alcohol. Dave's a good salesman. "Don't you trust your daughter?" he asks Mom.

"Yes, I just question if a nightclub is a good place for her."

"She'll be as safe here as she is in church. I'll see to it." Then Dave drives his point home. "I'll pick her up and drive her home. She won't even have to worry about transportation. And I'll pay her one dollar an hour." Waitresses don't make this kind of money—fifty cents an hour at best.

"Well, I guess she can try it if this is what she wants to do."

I think it's kind of strange that I've been off on my own in Rapid City and now she wants to decide what job I can take.

Dave picks me up for work at four on Thursday afternoon. The club will open for the first time on Friday and I'm to help get things ready.

In the kitchen I meet Ella, a frail, pale, sixty-something woman with stringy gray hair who will cook steaks, chicken, and shrimp to order. She's small, with deep-set colorless eyes that are surrounded by dark circles. Her skinny arms don't even look like they can lift a steak. I help Ella lug boxes to a table and open them. We stack spices, oils, sauces, gallons of pickles, and mayo on the shelves. We fill the fridge with cheeses, salad makings, and condiments. Ella teaches me how to make Roquefort salad dressing.

My new job is exciting for the first few days. People can only come in if they show a membership card. The card costs five hundred dollars so the clientele is people I've never seen before — rich businessmen from the area — Ranchers, civil engineers, legislators. It opens at five in the afternoon and closes at three in the morning. It's a place where men come to have affairs with floozies half their age who flaunt their wares with low-cut blouses, tight pants, and three-inch heels. I love the clothes they are wearing and wonder where they got them. The tips are very generous. The first night I get home just before dawn with forty dollars. *This beats Leonard's Café any day of the week.*

The second week, Ella watches Dave take advantage of me and never says a word. She sees him ply me with alcohol under the guise of my needing to know the names of specialty drinks when customers order them. She sees me so tipsy I can't stand up to him when he orders me to take off my blouse and remove my bra so he can inspect my "beautiful" breasts. She sits across from us in the red leather booth and never says a word.

Many nights after work Dave pours me a stiff drink, saying he wants my opinion on which alcohol is best and which he should stock up on. Some nights he drives me home so drunk I can hardly walk.

On several nights, Dave pulls off the road into some darkened tree-lined grove and tries to have sex with me. As drunk as I am, I fight off his fondling and hugs with every ounce of my strength and demand he take me home.

I'm not drinking any more, I decide. For weeks things go fairly well. Then Sara, Dave's skinny little blonde wife comes in. It's clear she thinks I'm a threat because she stares daggers at me. I want to tell her the truth, but I ignore it and rise above it.

As soon as she leaves, Dave pours me a screwdriver, then he makes me a Tom and Jerry, and after that he hands me a rum and coke. By the time I get home the next morning I'm so pie-eyed, I can barely stumble up the front steps to my front door and stagger the few feet to my room.

I'm not aware that Dave is making everybody believe he's having sex with me. To back up his story he gives me his car to drive. Sheila asks me if I am sleeping with Dave because Trixie, who comes to the club often, thinks this is why I'm driving the Lincoln. "No, I'm not! I swear I'm not!"

Sheila shakes her head. "Then you better stop driving his car, because it looks like you are."

After that when he drives me home and offers to let me keep the Lincoln for a day, I refuse.

Trixie is hired as a bartender. The first night she's there, Dave quickly switches his attention to her. But before he does, he says to me in front of a whole crowd of people at the bar, "Just because you've done me a few favors doesn't mean I owe you anything." The innuendo is plain. Embarrassed and humiliated, I run into the kitchen and lean on a counter. The doors are still swinging when he lurches in behind me. Picking up a butcher knife Ella just put down, I shake it at him thinking, *I could stab him so easy.*

"Don't come near me. I quit. I'm done with you," I rage.

Ella has walked away and is holed up in the walk-in cooler. She clearly doesn't want to be a witness to murder.

The blood drains from Dave's face. "Put the knife down," he says. "Please Evelyn, put the knife down. I stare at him drowning in fury. I'm torn I want to stab him and it takes all my effort to lay the knife on the counter.

Dave takes a deep breath and the color comes back to his face. "You can't quit, the place is full of people. Besides we're ten miles out in the country. How are you going to get home? Truce?" Now he sounds like he's begging.

I stomp back out to finish waiting on my customers. I even sit through a mortifying early morning breakfast at the Statesman with him and Trixie. *I can rise above this.* I'm tired, my feet hurt, my self-esteem is down the toilet as I watch dawn peek through the window of the café while Dave charms Trixie before delivering me to my house in sober silence.

Rolling out of bed at noon the next day, I tell my mom I quit. "Just wasn't for me. I don't like staying up all night and sleeping away my day."

That's a lie, I'm actually a night owl. I come alive at ten when most people are getting ready for bed and mornings are my enemy.

That night Dad says, "Did you quit or did you get fired?"

I just look at them, my parents, both so far removed from the reality of my life, so unaware of the aching, agonizing, humiliating pain I live with . . . so unbelievably ignorant.

Chapter Seventeen
Rejection and Salvation

My mom has a picture of herself taken when she was in her early twenties. It's a rose-shaded close-up of her beautiful femme-fatale face. Her seductive hooded eyes see something far off and her smile is a bit like the *Whistler's Mother* painting. Her bobbed 1920s hairstyle fits snuggly to her high cheekbones.

Since I won't be getting a senior picture, I make an appointment at Miller's Studio to have one taken of me to give her as an Easter present. On the day of the picture, I get my hair done. I've been letting it grow out and the beautician parts my hair in the middle, like Mom's, and does my eyes in soft blue shadow. I have to pay three dollars for this service but it's worth it.

At the studio I tell Mr. Miller it's my senior picture. He takes special care to get just what I want. A week before Easter I pick up an eight by ten and twelve billfold-size glamour shots. I buy a beautiful silver frame and love how my picture looks in the frame.

Mom will be delighted. I could never be as beautiful as she is, but this is not half bad.

Easter dawns and we're having a huge dinner. Ted's home and Mom puts out all his favorite foods. I'm thrilled to see him. Mike's home, too, and I don't even know where he's been.

It's not easy getting us all dressed up and out the door at the same time. The bathroom is the coveted space for the guys to adjust their ties and me to put on my make-up. Somehow we get out the door at ten. First Mom gets out her Brownie camera and captures us all for eternity. Mom and I are in new matching dresses, our handsome men in suits and ties. Dad looks spectacular in his new blue suit. We march to church together, sit lined up in the Jones pew, and listen to mom's beautiful soprano voice belt out *Jerusalem*. Shivers travel up my spine when she sings. Dad is probably right, she could have been a great opera star.

It's such a great day. Ted seems so grown up as he tells us tales of the air force base on San Clemente Island. He likes being stationed there, though he's disappointed he doesn't get to go overseas. He entertains us with word pictures about his barrack mates.

When Ted has to report back to his base, a part of my heart goes with him. But hanging on our living room wall is an eight by ten of him in his uniform. Mom oohed and awed over his picture when he gave it to her in a paper bag on Easter morning, which made my presentation of my beautifully wrapped, silver-framed picture anti-climactic.

I thought she'd put my picture on the wall right beside Ted's but she doesn't, not that day or the next, or the next. I find it on a shelf in her closet.

"Where are you gonna hang my picture?" I ask her one evening while we're doing the supper dishes.

"I don't like this picture of you. It doesn't look like you."

Don't let her know you care. Keep drying the dishes. Ignore this horrible feeling, it will go away.

"Still want to go to a movie tonight?" I ask her. We decided yesterday we were going to do this. "No, it's been a long day. I'm too tired." She finishes up the dishes in the sink and walks to the other room. *Well okay then, I guess I'll go see if Marcie's home.*

I don't say a word to Marcie about what happened with Dave and the nightclub. I don't want her to know how gullible and stupid I am.

Except for being broke, I actually enjoy not working anywhere. Hiding out from the world, I clean the house, do the laundry, and read every book I can get my hands on.

Every time I ask Dad for a dollar, he snorts. "What do you think I am? I s'pose you're too damn lazy to get out and make your own money. We feed you, and give you a roof over your head, isn't that enough? Have you ever paid a bill in your life?"

I'm sufficiently cowed even though I cook, clean, and iron his shirts. In fact, in any given week, I iron seventeen to twenty shirts for the men in this family.

To make some money, I take in ironing. For a month I stand at the ironing board all day long, three or four days a week, doing ironing for people who are only too glad to be freed of this chore. They pay me a dollar an hour and their clothes look perfect.

Marcie graduates without me and is getting married soon. I don't go to her graduation. I'm not up to the sneers I know I will get from the other graduates. I can't hack what their faces will say—"You're not good enough for us."

With Marcie starry-eyed and full of wedding plans, there's a chasm between us. Our worlds are vastly different now; even our dreams don't match anymore. It really hurts my feelings that I can't be her maid of honor because I'm not Catholic.

June 1 is my eighteenth birthday. Myrna and I celebrate our birthdays on the same day so this year we are having a party together. My mom, and Myrna's mom are planning a cook-out at the lake and we've invited all our friends. We'll have hamburgers, hot dogs, Mom's famous potato salad, baked beans, and two birthday cakes—a party to remember.

When I drag myself out of bed it's almost noon and Mom will be home for lunch soon. In the kitchen I look for something to fix for lunch and come up with a salad and macaroni and cheese. I slice some ham, make some coffee, and call it good. Bill and Bernie are here and Dad's even home for lunch. When Mom walks in the door we all sit down.

There are a couple of presents at the place where I sit but I'm not expecting much. I open the first one and it's a beautiful blue silk dress with ruffles and lace. There's a bottle of perfume from the boys, which I'm sure Mom gave them to give to me.

"Thanks everybody," I say, doing my best to sound grateful. I open the last box and a smaller box falls out. I open that one and gasp. It's a beautiful silver Bulova watch. The tiny silver face is set in a platinum casing with two tiny diamonds on both sides attached to a slender silver expansion band. I can't see because of the tears stinging my eyes.

"Thank you! Thank you!" I jump up from the table and hug first Mom and then Dad. I'm too excited to eat.

Mom and I, along with Bill and Bernie, meet Myrna, her mother, and Myrna's two little brothers at the lake for our cookout. I'm excited to show my watch to everyone. It's a beautiful evening, the sun's just heading toward the horizon, the lazy lake ripples at the shore from the boats that are chasing around near the middle, and there's a water-skier off in the distance.

We eat and walk the beach until about ten then our mothers go home with our little brothers, and the beer comes out and we party. Myrna's with Joe and I'm not with anyone. Our original fifteen guests have now turned into a crowd of about thirty or more. Some kids disappear in the woods, some sit on logs and talk, and some of us dance on the beach to a car radio.

I wake up and look at my new watch. It's seven am. *Where am I?* I look around and realize I'm in the back seat of Joe's car and it's parked in front of his parents' café. I check my clothes, everything is intact. *What happened?* The last thing I remember I was drinking beer on the beach, legally for the first time.

I can hear noises from the Sinclair station by the café. I look around and there's no one in sight so I climb out of the car and start walking the eight blocks toward home. There's no one out and about yet, but the town cop is sitting in his car on the corner in front of the Hop Scotch. He tips his hat to me and I wave back.

I sneak in the front door of our house and go to my room as quietly as possible. What will my mom say? I guess she didn't hear me because she says nothing.

§

Finally I get my old job back at Dan's toward the end of June and that puts an end to my joblessness. I still have enough free time to go to the lake, lie in the sun, and stop at A & W for root beer floats on the way home.

Esther breaks it to me at work that Pete's back from Korea.

Oh no. Pete is here. "What's that to me?" I say. *Never let them see you care.*

"Well," she says as she looks at me thoughtfully, "I thought you might want to know. He's been here for a week."

When I see him at the Saturday night dance, the pain of rejection stabs me in the heart. *Did he ever care for me or did he just say that so I'd have sex with him? I think he just said that. Oh well, I don't care. He's a jerk. Don't wear your heart on your sleeve.*

I'm dancing with Freddie, a sweet, kind, uncomplicated guy who is a fairly good dancer. Freddie and his sister are friends of mine. I think he'd like to be more than a friend, but he's not masculine enough to be anything more.

When the band takes a break, everybody either runs across the street to the bar to grab a drink or rushes to their cars where bottles or six-packs wait. A couple of stiff pulls from the bottle of vodka in Dave's car—horrible tasting stuff!—gives me the courage to dance like there's no tomorrow. There are three of us on this floor: Freddie, me, and my pride. I toss down a couple more drinks at the second break. Toward the end of the dance, emboldened by the false courage of intoxication, I walk over to Pete and stand weaving in front of him.

Pete doesn't look at me, just sits there and looks at his boots.

"Candy ass! You never wanted to marry me. You just wanted to have sex with me." Then I almost fall over, so I sit down and stare daggers at him.

Freddie rescues me and in a sweet voice says, "Come on, honey, I'm taking you home." Too bad I don't love Freddie, he's really a nice guy.

§

"I've decided to go back to high school." We're at supper and I search Mom's face to see what she thinks of this idea.

"Okay."

What is she thinking? Does it even matter?

Dad looks up, looks into my eyes and says, "It's about time you came to your senses. You've been a blockhead long enough."

I can tell he's pleased by the gruff way he says it.

Now that I'm a senior, life takes on a semblance of normalcy. I'm happy to have structure back in my life. The kids in my new class are a lot nicer and friendlier than in my other class. School is fun for the first time. I almost, sort of, feel I belong.

Because I'm eighteen, the legal age to buy beer, life with some of my schoolmates is one big party. We carry a gallon jug in the car, take it to the Eagle Bar, and I go in and have it filled from the tap, while the other kids wait in the car. We also buy Glugstike, a German beer that comes in a four-ounce can. It's horrible tasting stuff, but said to be the strongest beer available. We drink it through a straw because we've heard that a person can feel the effects faster that way — and we all agree there is no point in drinking if not to feel the buzz.

§

Wanda, a junior, is my new best friend and we spend a lot of time together. She lives in a small upstairs apartment in a house that's on my way to school. Her dad is wiry and very nice, and her mother is big, bosomy and kind and cleans other people's houses for a living.

Religious plaques hang all over the walls of their small apartment. Wanda says they go to the Baptist church. This is how she knows Billy Graham is coming to hold a revival in the big city hall across the river. Wanda wants to go and I agree to go with her.

Dad is actually home for supper on the night of the revival. As soon as Wanda gets to my house, I ask Dad, "Will you give us a ride to Pierre so we can go to the revival?"

He grunts and acts flustered, but I know he's not going to say no in front of Wanda. He actually cares what my friends think of him. This is a weapon I've used for years. Want something? Just get a friend to go with you when you ask.

An expectant hush fills the darkened, crowded auditorium. We are early enough to be seated about halfway to the stage. To my surprise Dad sits a few seats behind us.

George Beverly Shea and his gospel singers send tingles up my spine. Enthralled we listen to the singers with their hands outstretched as the melodies and words of *How Great Thou Art*, *The Old Rugged Cross*, and *Holy, Holy, Holy* draw us in.

I'm filled with a sense of awe as Billy Graham walks on the stage. I've never heard of the God he's talking about— One who loves us enough to send his Son to save us.

Yeah, but he killed his own Son. What kind of God does that?

I don't know Jesus, don't even want to, even though I learned all the songs in vacation Bible school. Songs like *Jesus Loves Me* and *This Little Light of Mine* are just words to me. But when Billy Graham finishes his impassioned plea and makes his altar call it's convincing and compelling. I find myself propelled out of my seat as if I'm picked up by another force. I line up in the front of the auditorium and Wanda's right beside me. Two guys take us off to a corner where they ask us our names, then pray with us.

"Evelyn," one guy says, "Do you want to give your life to Jesus?"

I sob out, "Yes."

"Then repeat after me, 'Jesus, I, Evelyn, come to you as a sinner. I ask you to forgive me and to wash me clean of all my iniquities. Jesus I want to follow you. I promise to worship and praise you. I relinquish my ways to follow your ways. In your name I pray. Amen.'" I repeat the words.

Wanda beside me is doing the same.

I'm thinking Dad, only a couple of seats behind us, must have seen us walk up to the front. *My dad is going to be so proud of me. I'm going to be a whole new person.*

When we come out the building there are only three or four cars left in the parking lot and Dad is furious. "Where the hell have you been? I've been sitting in this blasted car for an hour. I should've just drove off and left you here."

His cursing slashes my soul. "Dad, we went up for the altar call."

"Yeah, I bet you did. I bet you were out back fooling around with some boys."

"No, no, we weren't. I swear we weren't."

"Yeah, well I know you. You didn't go up for some damned altar call. Don't lie to me. You think I was born yesterday?"

Well, so much for Jesus. Why even try to be a good person, if my own dad doesn't believe me? If there actually is a God, and there must be, he hates me.

Silently fuming on the way home, I'm embarrassed that my dad blew up and cursed in front of Wanda. She doesn't mention it the next day, but by silent agreement we stop hanging out together.

I feel like a puppet dangling alone and crumpled from broken strings. It seems there are several of me.

At school I pretend to know who I am and I act like I know what I'm doing.

At home I'm the stubborn, wayward daughter who gets out of the house as often as possible.

At work I'm the efficient little waitress who can carry five plates of food in one trip.

At night with my new friends I'm the life of the party who drinks too much.

At church I'm the sinner who is beyond redemption.

Inside I feel completely, totally empty. Hollow. I'm a walking corpse that exists only because I don't want to hurt my family by killing myself.

Chapter Eighteen
Who Am I?

It feels strange to wake up in the morning not knowing who I really am or where I belong. Clearly, I don't belong in this family. Sometimes I feel six years old, sometimes I feel fifty. I wonder why I am here. Why was I ever born? Since I don't know who I am, I try on and adopt different personalities.

One week I'm Sandra Dee because I just saw her in a movie with Bobby Darin and she's sweet and unassuming. Thinking I'd rather be Marilyn Monroe, I put on tight sweaters and try to lower my voice and talk with my mouth open. I walk with an exaggerated wiggle and attempt to bat my eyes. But it's no good—I'd make a better Doris Day.

I emulate whichever actress I see, losing myself in their lives via movie magazines. Sometimes I read romance novels and put myself in the place of the femme fatale, but that never lasts long as the women depicted in the stories are dumb beyond comprehension. And yet . . . I too long for a happy ending so I plot, dream, and scheme to have one.

One evening my mom looks right at me, searches my face and says, "I don't know who you are."

Join the club, Mom.

I want to do as my dad suggested years ago and be a lady like my beautiful mom. I want to be sweet and kind and loving but I don't know how to get off this treadmill.

I live with Dad's words, the ones I started hearing before I was even old enough to know what they meant. "She's stubborn, scatterbrained, impudent, and disrespectful. She's contrary, headstrong, pigheaded and pertinacious." When I try to ignore him, or *rise above it,* he throws me the classic, "I hope when you get married you have five kids and they are all just like you." Another standard from his mouth is, "You'll be sorry when I'm dead."

Oh yeah? Don't count on it.

I fight him with the only weapon I have—one I inherited from mom—the silent treatment. No way I will let him know I hear him or even care what he thinks. If he comes in a room, I leave it. Not that he is ever home much. Sometimes I go for days without seeing him.

"I hate him," I tell my mom.

"No you don't. There is no room for hate in this house."

No room for love either.

§

In October Harold comes home on leave from the air force and shows up on my front step with a bouquet of flowers and I'm excited to see him. Trying to be stern, I say, "I thought we had a date the last time you were here and you never showed up." All the while, his cocky, jaunty smile is melting my heart.

"I'm sorry. Some friends threw a surprise good-bye party for me at the Eagle Bar. I guess I drank a little too much."

My stiff mood softens as I can see how that could happen and I decide to ignore his bad behavior.

"Would you like to go to the show tomorrow night?" he asks. "It's James Dean in *East of Eden*."

The movie fills me with angst and I feel rolled and swallowed whole in Dean's misery. Harold's comforting arms are around my shoulders as I drown in Dean's self-destruction. The raw disregard by the adults in his life fits easily with my own experience. I'm on another plane by the time it's over. My body seems possessed by the force of ugly, raw feelings and smashed breathless by a powerful love for James Dean.

I see Harold every day he's home. He waits for me when school gets out. We talk about his childhood, which was way worse than mine. He loves his mother but doesn't understand her behavior so we have this in common.

A rancher took pity on him and gave him his first job at the age of twelve. He dropped out of high school and spent a year in reform school. Then his mother took him by the hand to a recruiter's office and signed him up for the air force.

He says his dad, who he's named after, is, "the best damn horseman in South Dakota. Hell, there's no better horseman than my dad anywhere in the world." In the next breath he tells me, how his dad used to disappear for days, walk in unannounced after weeks of absence and beat Harold's sisters until they couldn't get out of bed for a week. At the age of five when he saw his dad coming, he'd climb a tree and sit in it for hours, waiting for his mother to come home or his dad to leave.

Every story sucks me further into his drama and my heart goes out to him. I feel as if we are one body against a brutal world. My life is a breeze in comparison with his.

My world rides on a rainbow. When Harold and I dance it's in perfect step. When we sit holding hands, we communicate without saying a word.

He takes me to his house to meet his family. His mother is a hard-working, soft-spoken woman who welcomes me with open arms. The rest of his family, not so much. Two younger brothers and two younger sisters look at me with suspicion. "What are you doing in our world?" they seem to say.

On the last night of his leave, we are snuggling in the car in front of my house. "I don't want you to go," I whisper into his neck. In his own sweet way he pulls back from our embrace and looks at me with an earnest expression on his face. Taking my face in his hands, he quietly asks, "If I asked you to marry me would you say yes?"

Caught off guard, I stare at him. But I quickly gather my wits enough to answer, "Yes."

"Then will you marry me?"

"Yes!" All the while I am thinking, *Does he really mean it? Is he going to be like Pete and change his mind when he gets back to his base?*

I am totally awed that someone wants to marry me. His attention thrills me, as well as his handsome devil-may-care attitude, dashing good looks, his love of dancing, laughter, and his love for his mother. Rational thoughts and decision-making go out the door as I think *Now I won't be a loser or a spinster*.

Before he leaves to go back to Casablanca in Morocco, we set a date for December so he can come home for Christmas. "I have to get permission from my first shirt and from the chaplain," he says, "but this won't be a problem."

Mom doesn't object when I tell her I'm getting married. She actually seems sort of excited. She seems relieved that I'm not pregnant and I don't have to get married.

Dad protests. "You need to go to college. How well do you know this Harold? Why haven't I ever met him?" He turns to Mom and asks, "Have you met him?

She shakes her head no.

"And you're going to let her marry some idiot who is not good enough for her? I suppose he's a Catholic too." In our family, being fat or Catholic have always been the two worst things anyone could be.

Dad grabs his hat, knocks over a lamp and slams out the door. Somewhere inside of me I feel sorry for him. There's an empty spot inside me he once filled. I long for the days when he and I were buddies. Even though his vile words often hurt me, I still think about his good days when he'd cuddle a little girl rejected by her too-busy mother.

Harold writes daily letters in his beautiful handwriting. Sometimes I get more than one letter a day telling me about faraway places and expressing his longing for home. I answer back and tell him about school and what my friends are doing. We write descriptions of movies we see and say what we like about them. Professing undying love to each other, we talk about how many kids we want to have. Six is a good number we agree, and plan that I will finish high school before joining him in Morocco.

By the middle of November the frequency of his letters drops way down. I'm starting to wonder if he changed his mind about getting married. Finally a letter comes saying he was on a mission he can't talk about. "Sorry for the lapse in mail."

I spend hours planning a candlelight Christmas wedding. Mom says we can go shopping in Huron to find some of the things we need. We get up at six, and as quietly as possible make a thermos of coffee, and cram cinnamon rolls, ham sandwiches, and fruit into a bag, and we are off to drive two hours to be at the stores when they open.

Walking out the door, Mom pulls a hundred dollar bill out of her pocket to transfer to her purse. "Dad gave me this to spend on you." My mom doesn't normally gush, but right then she comes close in her excitement. Suddenly we are co-conspirators.

In the one bridal store available we order crinkly onion-paper invitations with silver embossed writing, making sure to have all the information just right:

> Mr. and Mrs. Lon Jones request the honor of your presence
> at the candlelight wedding ceremony
> of their daughter Evelyn Jones
> to
> Airman First Class Harold J Copper.
> First Congregational Church

Fort Pierre, South Dakota,
December 27, 1956, 7 p.m.
Reception to follow in the church basement.

The invitations when printed will be mailed directly to our house and come with matching thank-you notes.

Our next stop is Geyerman's where we plow through racks and racks of attractive dresses, skirts, blouses, and coats. "You need a going-away dress." Mom holds up a soft beige dress with ruffles around the high neck that cascade down the front and a flowing chiffon skirt.

This is not me. This is her. She's the ruffles person. "How about this one?" I hold up a sharp turquoise gaberdine batwing-sleeved dress with a slim hip-hugging skirt.

When I try it on she says, "It fits like it was made for you." The dress is expensive at eight dollars and ninety-eight cents, but into the hands of the clerk it goes. We ooh and ah over a filmy, ocean-blue lace-trimmed negligee set, with a filmy, see-through knee-length peignoir floating over a sheer spaghetti-strap nightgown. This is all piled on the counter with a black velvet mother-of-the bride outfit, and a white satin pillbox hat.

In the fabric store next door we buy yards of white frothy net that Mom can attach to the pillbox hat to make a veil and two yards of Chantilly lace." If this is too much, I can always edge pillowcases with it," Mom says.

Florence, one of Mom's friends, is going to make me a bolero top, with fingertip sleeves, to go with the fanciful, strapless, white-tulle gown with the beaded bodice that I found at Freda's French Fashions. At fifty dollars, the dress was one of the most expensive in the store.

On the ride home from Huron, we are tired but triumphant. We spent the whole hundred dollars. *Mom is actually fun sometimes*, I think. Walking in the house loaded down with bags, it's back to earth as the smell of hamburger along with fried potatoes with onions hits us. Dad and the boys are just finishing supper.

Though I don't particularly like Harold's sister, Dee Dee, I ask her to be my maid of honor in an attempt to please Harold. Her husband, Burt, is Harold's best man. A girl, Diane, from the senior class will sing *Because* and *I Love You Truly*. Mom arranges for the ladies of the church to provide lunch and asks Bertha to bake a three-tiered wedding cake with a bride and groom topper. Mike and Bill will be ushers, and Bernie and my little cousin Charity will be candle lighters.

Relatives are answering the call. Aunt Pearl and her family are coming, Aunt Blanche and Uncle Henry will be here, and Aunt Helen and her husband and their kids will make it.

A few days before Christmas, Dad gets on his pride horse and springs into action. It suddenly dawns on him that our living room needs to be repainted and the ceiling needs to be patched before our company arrives.

"Now?" Mom acts incredulous.

"Yes, now, and I think we should paint the dining room too."

"Then I'll have to buy new drapes."

In our house there's a big difference between what is seen and what actually is going on. I'm pretty sure Mom in her own sweet way wondered out loud if Dad's relatives might think our house is a little run down.

"How are we going to get all this done?" Mom asks.

Dad already has the answer. "I'll get John Temple to start on the ceiling tomorrow. I think he'll help with the painting too."

The details of the wedding are in place. I'm waiting for the groom to ride in on his white horse, a.k.a. airplane.

Mom and Dad have stopped painting for the night and fallen into bed exhausted. I overhear Dad say. "What if all this is for nothing? What if he doesn't even show up?"

"Don't even say that."

"Well, we don't know this guy and I just don't want her to get hurt again."

So Dad did know how hurt I was over Pete. Maybe he does love me.

"Sure wish Ted could've have gotten a leave to come home for Christmas," Mom says softly.

Christmas Eve we have our usual oyster stew and chili, but no ice cream this year. Dad's still finishing hanging the new drapes in the living room. It's a mad rush to get done before church at ten.

Christmas Day is an unusual sixty degrees, not the ten degrees below zero it could be. I open my presents, and the main one is a small, sandy-colored Samsonite suitcase to hold my new trousseau. We will be leaving immediately following the reception for the luxurious St. Charles Hotel in Pierre.

Still no word from Harold and I'm getting nervous. I step out the front door leaving the deafening noise in the living room behind me with kids yelling, dogs barking, and Dad squishing wrapping paper in a box with his feet. Not only this, the living room reeks of fresh paint. Leaning against the huge elm tree that hovers over the sidewalk in front of our house, I light up a cigarette. I stopped hiding my smoking from my parents at least a year ago.

A car rolls up, Harold jumps out and envelops me in a bear hug and relief washes over me like milk poured from a bucket. *He's here!* Almost before I know what's happening, he drops to his knees and puts a diamond on my finger. The diamond, set in a gold band, looks huge. Later I learn it's a one-fourth carat and cost $295 dollars. Harold picks me up and twirls me around, and we are kissing, laughing, hugging, all giddy with excitement.

Just then I notice from my perch on a cloud that Aunt Helen and her brood are just pulling up for Christmas dinner. They start pulling boxes out of the trunk and everybody carries something My cousins have their arms full of the presents Santa brought them this morning.

Harold and I stay out in the front yard until Mike comes to say dinner is ready, then I drag Harold in the house to meet everybody. The big table where the adults sit is piled high with turkey, dressing, mashed potatoes, gravy, a huge fruit salad covered in fresh whipped cream, green gelatin salad with cottage cheese, creamed corn casserole, and home-baked rolls.

On the buffet are apple, pumpkin, mincemeat, and pecan pies, cookies, Chinese chews (mom's favorite bars), fudge, and divinity. Suddenly I'm starving.

From the children's table is in the kitchen, I can hear clamoring of the kids unrestricted by adults until they are told to come join us in prayer. We stand around the dining room, hold hands, and say the Lord's Prayer.

Harold is shy at the table and says little, but I can tell Mom likes him.

The day after Christmas, Aunt Pearl, along with Bobbie, Larry, and Ray arrive. Then Aunt Blanche, Gail and Uncle Henry come. They bring hominy grits, home-ground sausage, farm- fresh eggs, potatoes for frying, sweet watermelon pickles, and canned stuffed peppers (my favorite), for our wedding-day breakfast.

December 27, 1956 is a beautiful, uncharacteristically warm sixty-five degree day. "God is smiling on you," Mom says. She has a firm belief that God uses weather to reward or punish people, among a number of his other methods of getting your attention.

The day flies by. I can't see or talk to Harold—bad luck for the bride and groom to see each other on their wedding day. Before I know it, it's time to put on my dress, find a bag for my veil and white satin shoes, check my make-up and get my picture taken with Mom's Brownie camera.

Aunt Helen, Aunt Dorothy, and Aunt Della with their families will meet us at the church. Mom and the boys pile into Aunt Pearl's car and lead a caravan of people there. Dad and I are to ride together. Dad opens the door for me and I climb in the car carefully arranging my yards of frothy white tulle, holding the sack with the shoes and veil. Dad hands me the white Bible with an orchid arranged on top, cautiously closes my door then walks around to his side of the car.

Suddenly I'm gripped with a horrible feeling of impending doom. Everything in me is saying, *Stop, stop! Don't do this! I don't want to do this.* I look at Dad. What would he say if I said I had changed my mind? What would all those people waiting at the church say? I feel panicky. A voice deep within me taunts me saying, *You'll be sorry. You'll be sorry. You'll be sorry.*

A railroad track runs between us and the church. When I hear a train whistle my thoughts are jumbled. *Maybe we'll get hit by a train. That would be a great excuse for calling off this wedding. What's the matter with me? I love Harold. Am I having a premonition as I so often do? I'll just ignore it and it will go away.*

As we wait in silence for the train to go by, I look sideways at Dad who is looking handsome in his new dark suit, gray felt hat, a gleaming white shirt and a new red Christmas tie held in place by a Black Hills gold tie tack.

Why are you letting me do this? Why didn't you say no?

The door of the church is open and it is full. There are shouts of talking and laughter. My panic of a few moments earlier about getting married is gone. I'm relieved to learn the groom is already here.

Ducking past the crowd in the entryway, we head down the stairs to the basement where Mom is greeting all her family. The tables are covered with white linen tablecloths with Christmas decorations in the center. The wedding cake at the head table is a vision. All the family except me and Mom and Dad head upstairs where Mike and Bill are busy finding seats for everyone. I'm sad that Ted can't be here; Marcie can't be here either. *Damn Catholic priests. Shake it off, rise above it, you'll be just fine.*

The music starts and Mom walks down the aisle on my brother Mike's arm, looking stunning in a simple black velvet sheath dress and black pill box hat surrounded by a cloud of black veiling.

The piano switches from Christmas music to *Here Comes the Bride* and Dad holds out his arm. He's doing his best to hide that he's crying.

Crying? My Dad is crying?

Brushing his eyes with the back of his hand, he walks me up the aisle. When the minister says, "Who gives this woman to be married to this man?" Dad is barely audible as he croaks out "I, her father do," what the minister told him to say.

Originally, Dad said, "There is no way in hell I'm giving my daughter away."

But then Mom said, "You have to. What will it look like if you don't?"

So Dad agrees because she's the boss.

The reception plays out like a movie. It's as if I'm standing outside myself and watching the bride smile, laugh, and lie through her teeth. "Oh, yes," I say, "as soon as we get back from Africa, we're going to buy a house."

Following the church reception, we stop at my house so I can change my clothes and pick up the suitcase I've had packed for two weeks. On the way to the hotel we stop at the Legion Club, where Harold's whole family is celebrating and take our first drinks as a married couple. Harold's twenty-one and can drink whatever he wants. Now that I'm his wife, so can I.

The honeymoon is an incredible adventure in new experiences. I'm suddenly terrified. I'm just a befuddled, eighteen-year-old who has had years of saying "No," dodging perverts, fighting teenage boys off, and now suddenly sex is okay?

It's not only okay, it's expected. Alcohol eases the way. Harold says no hurry, we have the rest of our lives. *No wonder I love him so much*, I think.

Enjoying long lazy days in bed with room service and nowhere to be is a completely new experience for me. Harold is a thoughtful, gentle, shy lover. We end up laughing until we cry over our clumsy attempts to act like we know what we are doing. I'm in la-la land. Who shall I be? Elizabeth Taylor from *A Place in The Sun*, or Marilyn Monroe from *How to Marry a Millionaire*?

When we come up for air, we drive out to Harold's house to pick up some more clothes for him. Burt gives me a hard time. "It only hurts for a little while," he says, obviously referring to sex.

I pipe back at him, "Isn't that the name of a song?" I'm trying desperately to be clever but it's a lost cause in the end as I'm just so embarrassed about the whole sex thing.

When the honeymoon money runs out, we go back to my house and stay in my room for a couple of days until it's time for Harold to go back to his new base in Africa. I take him to the train station by myself, kiss him goodbye at midnight and drive home alone sobbing.

At home I slip into my room still sobbing. *Doesn't Mom hear me crying? Would it be too much for her to put her arms around me and comfort me? Yeah, well that's not going to happen now.* In my family when you cry, you cry alone. Lost and lonely I cry myself to sleep.

Harold's gone and I feel empty without him. Everything returns to what it was before the wedding. I spend the first day of his absence writing thank-you cards for the stacks of presents lined up on a wall in my bedroom.

Chapter Nineteen
A Milestone

It's my first day back at school. The day has a surreal feeling even before Linda, the office clerk, stops me in study hall. "Mr. Krout wants to see you in the office" she whispers in my ear.

Our self-important, chubby, checked-suited principal is waiting for me behind his desk. He looks up. "Close the door."

What now?

His words tumble out. "I sorry, but you will not be allowed to come back to school now that you are married. Some of the other kids' parents have called me. They don't want their girls going to school with a married woman. Now that you are sexual and all, they're afraid you'll lead their daughters astray."

What? Dumbfounded and speechless, I walk back up the stairs. While the other kids are still in class, I put on my winter coat, and weighed down by books and the blow of the principal's words, I stagger the six blocks home. It's laughable that some parents think I'll be a bad influence on their innocent daughters now that I'm married. Do they think their daughters live under a rock? Do they think their daughters don't know the facts of life? Are they nuts?

Lurching into the house, I spill my books on the living room floor. Dad's sitting at the table as he's doing the swing shift at the capitol today.

"The principal kicked me out of school for getting married," I tell him.

He snorts, grabs his coat, and charges out the front door. About thirty minutes later he walks back in. "Pick up your stuff. I'm driving you back to school."

Triumphantly, I grab my coat. "What did you say to him?"

"I said if my married daughter can't go to school, then your married basketball star can't either. Fair is fair."

Wow, my Dad is tough. He probably showed him his fists too.

Meekly I say, "Thank you."

Back in the office the principal pretends like nothing happened. When I say "I'm back" he looks at me like *why wouldn't you be?*

§

I need another credit and the only class I'm interested in taking is woodshop. I walk into a classroom filled with the smell of sawdust in the air—and ten boys. Mr. Manson, the shop teacher, is a frail, pasty-faced man who looks about eighty years old. His blue plaid shirt is faded and his pants hang off his scrawny frame. He looks at me with a shocked expression on his face and says in a demanding tone of voice, "What are you doing here? Girls do not take shop!"

"I signed up for shop. I want to learn how to make a coffee table for my mother."

"Well, you can't be in here," he says as he rushes out the door.

I stay where I am.

When he comes back, he says, "Take a seat."

He probably went to the principal who doesn't want another run in with my dad.

When Mr. Manson calls my name for roll call he doesn't look at me. During class he doesn't help me learn anything, or show me how to use the power tools. I pick out the simplest blueprint I can find in the catalog, buy some oak for the coffee table and Jake and Mitch help me as much as they can while doing their own projects. If I ask Mr. Manson a question about measuring or cutting the boards, he says, "Girls don't cut boards" or "Girls can't measure things right." When my floppy, lop-sided coffee table is varnished and done, it's pitiful.

Jake tells me, "It's not too bad for a girl."

My appreciation and admiration for Jake knows no bounds. His kindness makes my knees buckle.

"It could have been nice if Mr. Manson would have helped me."

"Yeah," Jake says, "he sure is mean to you." Tears in my eyes, embarrassed, I duck my head. *I will not cry. Funny when someone is mean to me I can spit in their face, but when someone is nice I cry.*

§

The only thing different in my life now than before the wedding is that I have money from an allotment that Harold sends from his pay every month—a whole $134.00!

"One thing about Evelyn," my mom says, "if she has money everybody has money." She's right, I buy food for friends who are broke, gifts for my brothers, and even pay a light bill or two. Mostly though I buy stuff for Mom.

I'm pretty much staying at home at night like a married woman should. But I do have a small part in the junior/senior play, and I'm helping with the scenery too. As part of a crew working toward something special, it feels good to belong. The night of the production, I look out through the slit in the curtains at the front of the stage and see a gymnasium full of people, including my mom, dad, and brothers.

I'm afraid of humiliating myself by forgetting the few lines I have in scene two. I walk on the stage in a cold sweat and when it's my time to speak, the lines come out in a different voice from normal, but the words are all there.

At home I ask Mom, "What did you think of the play?"

"Your acting leaves a lot to be desired."

I'm sorry I asked.

I work at Dan's Café a couple of nights a week, but mostly I'm home at night. I spend my time writing letters to Harold, eating fried onion rings with Mom—our favorite. I run down to the café and order take-out every Friday night and play games with Bernie. If Dad's home, we play cards, Canasta, Pinochle, or Whist. The four or five of us (if Bill's home) are really competitive when it comes to playing cards.

Sometimes I stop on my way home from Dan's and stare in the window of the hardware store, along with the rest of the crowd, at a Philco console television set playing programs like *Our Miss Brooks*. I dream about how nice it would be to have one of those.

Rose, one of my friends in school, tells me that some of the kids are taking bets on whether I'm pregnant or not. She asks me point-blank. "Did you have to get married?"

"No."

With a quizzical look on her face, she asks, "Then why would you?"

"I'm going to Africa as soon as school is out, isn't that a good enough reason?"

We got married at Christmas so Harold would have time to do the necessary paperwork for me to join him. Then in a letter Harold tells me, "The air force says you can't come here unless I re-up or I will have to pay your way. I'm not reenlisting so guess you'll have to live at home until I get out in October."

§

I have no clue what's happening in school until Mrs. Lear, my English teacher, calls me aside. "You are one-half a credit short of graduating. You better go see Mrs. Carol and ask her about it."

Surprised, I thank her. The snafu with Mrs. Carol involves some unfinished work from my junior year. "Please let me do the work. I have to graduate." She sets it up so I can stay after school and finish the missing work. You never know who your friends are. Mrs. Lear, of all my teachers, is the one I think likes me the least.

At last finals are complete. I feel I did a pretty good job on all my tests. The reward is Skip Day for the entire senior class. The class votes to do an overnight trip to the Black Hills using money we've made from school carnivals to pay for the hotel rooms. Cars are lined up and we take off in a caravan with Mr. Krout as our only chaperone. After we check into the motel, we go to the VFW Club for burgers and all the alcohol we can drink. Some of us are toast before midnight.

There are four girls to each room, and the boys are bunked together down the hall. I'm spending most of the night vomiting up cherries from the many Tom Collins I swilled. The other kids are chasing up and down the hall, in and out of the rooms, with booming voices, playing tricks on each other. I go outside to sit under the stars. Jake comes out to talk to me. We talk about what we're going to do now that school is out and I tell him how much I miss my husband. On the way home the next day, our caravan of eighteen high-spirited, mostly hung-over seniors stops every chance we get to invade restaurants, climb hills, and take pictures. Graduation is just a few days away. Life is good.

It's a soft, warm morning and I'm on my way to school to pick up my cap and gown and report card. My footsteps sound hollow in the empty hall and there is no clerk in the office. Fat, bald-headed Mr. Krout comes out from behind his desk with beads of sweat on his face and closes his office door behind me. "Here's your report card and it's all Ds. I'm not sure I should let you graduate."

He waits a moment for this to sink in. "I could fix this for you. I could change these Ds to As right here, right now." He has a peculiar look on his face and a leer in his eye. "If you just do for me what you do for your husband when he's home, I'll make sure you graduate."

The shock keeps me silent for a moment. Then I think, *You pervert, you crazy, good-for-nothing pervert.* Squaring my shoulders, I glare at him. "No thanks!" I start out the door without my report card.

He follows me. "Don't forget this," he says and hands me the brown envelope.

In the car I sit in shock. I don't know what to do. *Who should I tell about this? Can he actually keep me from graduating?*

I drive up the hill to Glenda's house. She's the most level-headed senior girl I know. We've done a few things together because her boyfriend is a good friend of Harold's. We have coffee in her room while I explain what Mr. Krout, Old Crow as we call him, said. She's shocked and sympathetic but she doesn't know what to do about it either. In the end, I fall back on my best resource—ignore it and it will go away.

Graduation comes and my apprehension is growing. To keep from thinking about Mr. Krout's behavior, I buy carnations in school colors as presents for everyone in the senior class. The kids are surprised. Three of them have even bought presents for me.

The first thing I do when the ceremony is over is look to see if my diploma is signed. A huge sigh of relief escapes me. It is signed! I made it!

Some of the senior girls are crying and hugging each other. *Are you kidding me? I am so happy to be done with this.*

All of us who drink are off to party all night. I wish Harold could have seen me graduate.

Chapter Twenty
Preparing for the Future

Some of the girls from my class are getting ready to go to college, but there is no money for college at our house. Mom suggests I try a three-month business college in Omaha, Nebraska.

The advertisement in our weekly newspaper says:

> The National School of Business, a community college opportunity for girls, offers a quality education in secretarial skills, or airline clerk expertise. Very affordable at $900 for the three-month school. Next class starts June 10, 1957, ends August 16, 1957. Every student guaranteed a job at graduation. Call or write . . .

I'm thinking this might be the perfect way to spend the summer since Harold won't be home until October. I like the idea of being a clerk for the airlines. I always wanted to be a stewardess but I'm not built right. In order to be a stewardess a girl has to be a minimum of five-feet, eight-inches tall, thin, and single. I fail on all counts. But I could sell airline tickets and meet a lot of people that way.

It's already May 30th so I need to hurry. "Mom, can I make a long-distance call on the phone to talk to somebody at the school?" I ask.

"Yes, but try not to talk to more than three minutes. You know how expensive long-distance calls are." Mom refuses to talk long distance on the phone to anybody for more than three minutes because Bell Telephone charges fifty cents a minute for every minute over the standard three.

When I get the business college on the line, I ask for information and they are only too happy to help. The woman on the other end says, "Did you graduate from high school?"

"Yes, a week ago."

"Good. Do you have three references you can send us?"

"Yes, do you want them right now?"

"No, just mail them with your check for $900."

I am relieved that she doesn't want them now, but wonder who would give me a reference. Not my high school principal, for sure.

"Once we receive your money we will find you a place to live. We have private homes here that our girls stay in. I will call around and see where I can find you a room."

She sounds very nice and the school sounds intriguing, but where am I going to get the money? I decide to go talk to our banker, Bill Berry. He seems like a nice old man, and is always friendly when I deposit my allotment check. I put on my best clothes and fix my hair before I go to the bank because Mom always says, "Bankers only loan money to people who don't look like they need it."

Years of being told "Children are to be seen and not heard" have made me terrified of authority. Most of the time I am tongue-tied around the adults I respect. I feel very strange walking into the bank with its floor-to-ceiling log walls that smell like lemon oil. Off in a corner there is a tall wooden shelf with a bottle of black ink sunk in the inkwell and a quill pen in a holder beside it. The floor of polished oak boards creaks as I walk across it. I'm nervous as I step up to the teller window.

"Is Mr. Berry available?"

"Yes, he's here."

"Can I talk to him?" Boy, do I want a cigarette right now.

"Just a minute. I'll see."

Nancy walks back to an inner office and in a couple minutes she comes back.

"He can see you. Follow me."

I square my shoulders, and suck in my stomach, take a deep breath, and follow her.

Mr. Berry's office has pine walls and a huge picture window that looks out over the sidewalk and across to the post office. His walls are covered with paintings by Harvey Dunn, South Dakota's most famous artist. The banker is a nice looking old man with gray hair, kind blue eyes behind wire-rimmed glasses and a paunch. His gold cuff links practically shout money.

He comes out from behind his huge wooden desk, and shakes my hand. "Good morning, Evelyn, what can I do for you?

He knows my name! Taking a deep breath and hoping not to make a fool of myself I say, "I've decided I want to go to business college in Omaha." It takes some effort but I get the words out.

"I think that's great, how can I help?" Mr. Berry is all smiles and encouragement.

"I need to borrow $900 to pay the tuition."

"Well, I'm sure we can arrange that. How are you going to make the payments?"

"I get $134 a month from my husband in the air force."

"Do you think you can pay $50.00 a month until it's taken care of?"

"Yes, I can manage that."

"Since your husband isn't here, your dad's going to have to sign the papers with you. We don't loan money to women without a co-signer. I'll get the papers ready and you bring your dad in."

I walk out of the bank feeling triumphant. But now I have to go find Dad. I dread having to do this because even though I know he will sign the loan, I also know I'm going to have to listen to a lecture before he does.

Dad blusters and huffs and blusters some more as I knew he would. "Are you sure this is what you want to do? Or is it like that shorthand school that cost your mother and me $400? Are you going to get there and drop out? Can I trust you to make the payments?" And finally, "Why do you want to do this anyway?"

"Dad, I don't want to be a waitress all my life."

"Why can't you go over to the capitol and work for the state like all the other high school graduates do?"

"You are the one who always wants me to better myself." This is my punchline and it works.

The next morning we walk into the bank and Dad signs the papers. After he signs them, Mr. Berry shakes his hand. "I bet you're really proud of your daughter, Lon."

Dad stands up straight and answers, "Yes, I am."

Mom meets a couple of girls in the store where she works who tell her they live and work in Omaha. Mom knows their parents because they live in Fort Pierre and shop in the store a lot. She tells the girls I am going there to business school and they give her their phone number and promise her they will keep tabs on me.

The night before I am to leave for school, some of my friends throw a party for me, and even Dorothy and Cleve who are home on vacation are there. I don't know who is buying the alcohol but there is lots of it and the party gets rowdy. We go out to a vacant house that belongs to somebody's parents. A long table made out of wooden boards spread over two sawhorses has Jello, potato salad, baked beans, pickles, baloney lunch meat, bread, mustard, ketchup, and a big chocolate cake.

I don't eat much. My opinion has always been if I'm going to drink, I'm going to drink, and if I'm going to eat,

I'm going to eat. The two don't fit together, otherwise why drink?

The next thing I know someone yells, "Food fight!" and there is food flying all over. I don't want to get anything on my clothes so I step out outside and Dorothy joins me. When we go back inside there is food all over the floor, the walls, and mustard and ketchup are dripping from the ceiling. Looking at it makes me feel sick.

"We better get out of here; I have a bus to catch." I'm tugging at Cleve's shirt on one side and Dorothy is on his other side.

Dorothy and Cleve drive me home to pick up my bag and my suitcase, which is packed and ready on our front porch. In my purse is the phone number for the girls in Omaha, whom I've never met. I'm to connect with them when I get there.

At the bus depot, the 5 a.m. Jack Rabbit bus is pulling up to the depot as Dorothy and Cleve drop me off. I climb aboard, still feeling the alcoholic buzz, but able to navigate the aisles and find a seat. I make myself as comfortable as possible for the eight-hour ride ahead of me. Since I've been up all night, I sleep almost all the way, waking up with a stiff neck and a horrible headache.

By the time we get to Omaha, I desperately need a bathroom so I charge off the bus to take care of business and then rush back to the bus to grab my suitcase. A well-dressed man in a three-piece suit, with a colorful tie, walks up to me. He's probably in his fifties, not bad looking, with a little gray hair around the temples.

"Pardon me, miss."

He's sort of in my path so I stop.

"Have you ever thought about being a model?"

I respond with a resounding, "No."

"Too bad, you're so pretty. I'm an agent and I would have no trouble getting you a job as a model."

I brush past him. I may be naïve, but I'm not that stupid. No one in their right mind would consider me model material.

The man follows me to the pay phone and asks, "Do you live here?" I ignore him but he persists. "Can I give you a ride somewhere?"

I drop a dime in the pay phone slot and dial Rachael's number. "I will be there in about a half hour," she says. It's been a long ride and I'm starving so a nickel gets me a Butterfinger candy bar from a vending machine and another nickel buys me a coke.

Rachael and her friend Berniece show up as promised and I tell them what happened. "See that man standing there by the coke machine?" I point at the guy in the three-piece suit. "He tried to pick me up when I got off the bus."

Rachael says, "Yeah, those kind of guys hang around the bus depot all the time. They pick up unsuspecting girls and boys and promise them jobs and all kinds of other things. They mostly pick on runaway kids who have nowhere to go. Then no one ever hears from the kids again. They call it white slavery."

I knew it. I knew he was a pervert. I feel sorry for the kids who fall for his tricks and wish I could help them somehow.

"Are you hungry?" Rachael asks me.

"Yes, starving."

"Okay, let's get you something to eat before we take you to the house where you are staying."

While I'm gobbling down a hamburger and french fries, I dig through my purse and pull out the address of the private home where I am to room with five other girls for the next three months. Rachael says, "Oh that's in a nice neighborhood in the historical district."

It's nine o'clock on Sunday evening when Rachael and Bernice and I pull up in front of Mrs. Stern's home. The sign out front says, "Historical Queen Anne home, built in 1896." It's a white house with a big porch with a railing that runs along one side of the house and it looks huge to me. Rachael walks to the front door with me.

When Mrs. Stern opens the door, she's cross. "I gave up on you and went to bed." Shaking her head in disapproval, she invites me to come in.

I turn to Rachael and give her an awkward hug. "Thank you so much."

Mrs. Stern shows me to a dingy basement with concrete walls. A large room holds a kitchenette, and six single beds. Another room that used to be a storage room now contains a shower near the washer and dryer. At the end of an even darker hallway is a coal room with a small window near the ceiling where the coal is funneled in from a truck backed up to the house. This is what Mrs. Stern feeds the furnace that stands near the laundry room. The furnace makes a strange noise and I can smell coal dust in the air.

Audrey, another student, is already here as her parents dropped her off this afternoon. "I'm so glad you're here. It's creepy down here by myself." She tells me the other four girls will come tomorrow after the orientation at school. I'm so glad I don't have to sleep in this dungeon by myself.

The next morning is my first experience of taking a city bus. We walk to the corner and wait for it and it almost feels surreal to climb aboard. I'm captivated by sights of the city, *I can't believe I'm here.* When we go through the formalities of signing up for school, sitting in the huge gathering room for the orientation, I am completely amazed at the number of girls who are here with their parents. My parents never even accompanied me to register for the first grade.

Training to be an airline clerk is complicated. I learn to punch cards with a coding machine that ultimately gives information on the destination of the flying customer along with the cost of the ticket. We not only have to learn how to code these tickets, we have to learn how to read them. I'm also studying basic secretarial skills, such as the proper way to answer the telephone, type a business letter, and how to always put the customer first.

My roommates turn out to be fun and agreeable. It's like a three-month slumber party except they all live close enough to go home on the weekends and I can't. We each have to furnish our own food. Many times we are hungry because one or more of us has run out of money for groceries. We buy dried chicken noodle soup in a pouch for ten cents, and often that is what we have for supper.

Sometimes one of the girls will bring food from home when she comes back on Sunday, but that's usually gone by Monday evening.

At the end of my third week of school, I go downtown to the Grande Hotel on Dodge Street and apply for a waitress job in their prestigious dining room where the manager hires me on the spot for twenty-five cents an hour plus tips. I'm told that the cheap wage is because of the great tipping clientele. He's right, wealthy people come here. I work a couple of nights a week and Saturdays and I never go home with less than 10.00 or twenty dollars in tips. At the end of the week, my paycheck is usually only four or five dollars.

I can take a bus to work, but I always take a cab home, because both the school and Mrs. Stern repeatedly warn us to "never be out at night alone."

Almost every night Cecil our cook sends me home with leftovers. I really like him. He laughs and jokes and is good to all the waitresses. It's my first real exposure to someone who actually moved to the United States from Africa.

I am extremely lonesome for Harold and for my family, especially on Sundays when I'm in the dismal basement apartment alone. I'm so lonely that suicide even crosses my mind. During these times, I writes letter after letter to my Mom and to Harold, telling them about school, about my new job, and about the wealthy people I'm rubbing elbows with at the Grande Hotel.

When Sunday evening comes and the girls start filing back in to our room, I'm so very relieved.

One Saturday after all the girls are gone, I am home from work early in the evening. Mrs. Stern calls me to come upstairs. I stand in her kitchen and listen as she reads me the riot act. "You girls are pigs living in a pig sty. Everything down there is a mess and I want it cleaned up today!"

I look at this small elderly woman with her short, wispy gray hair flying in every direction and a dowager's hump on her back. I know what to call it because every time we see a woman with a hump at the top of her back, my mother exclaims, "I hope I never get a dowager's hump like that."

"Why are you yelling at me?" I ask her. "There are five other girls living here."

Pointing her finger at me, she says, "You are the oldest and the most responsible. I know if I tell you it will get done."

Wow, talk about a backhanded compliment, and I'm not the oldest.

When the girls come back on Sunday night the kitchen is spotless and the area around my bed is as neat as I can make it. Mrs. Stern has checked it and given her approval.

August 16, 1957 finally arrives. A small graduation ceremony takes place on Friday evening. I'm packed and ready to catch an early morning bus for home. I'm so homesick I can hardly stand it. The school, true to its promise, has found all of us jobs. I am scheduled to go to Washington D.C. to work in the Pentagon as a receptionist along with Audrey. My grades, though straight Cs, were not good enough to work for an airline. I'm fine with that. The thought of moving to Washington D.C. is exciting and

Harold says he will be happy to move there when he gets home in October.

I'm thrilled to be home with my family again. When I announce that I'm moving to D.C. to work in the Pentagon, Dad is visibly upset. He doesn't say much for a couple of days then he plays the surgery card. "I've decided to have the surgery on my gallbladder at the end of September. I sure would like for you be here when I do this. You know I might not make it through it. That's why I put it off until you could be here."

I know when I'm defeated. "Okay, Dad. I won't go."

"Good. That's a terrible place for a young girl to go by herself."

The next day I go to Dan's Café and ask for a job. That's where Harold finds me working when he comes home on October 12th. When I see him walk into the café, I am so excited I can't contain my screams. Dan comes out of the kitchen and says, "You can leave, Evelyn. Take the day off. Hell, take the week off."

We buy a small airstream trailer home for two hundred dollars and park it in my dad's trailer park behind our house. Harold gets work as a gravel truck driver for some friends of his who have a concrete business across the river in Pierre, South Dakota. Then we decide we will move to Denver, Colorado right after Thanksgiving. My friend Sheila and her husband live there and they keep telling us to come there because there are lots of jobs and many wonderful things to do.

The night before Thanksgiving, we go out with some friends and drink, dance, and celebrate life. But when one of Harold's friends asks me to dance, Harold picks up his change, his cigarettes, and his jacket and says, "Come on, we are going home." His face looks stormy.

"Ah, Harold," his friend says, "I wasn't making a play for your wife, I just wanted to dance with her." Harold gives him a curt nod, takes my hand and practically pulls me out the door.

"What's the matter with you?" I ask.

"I saw the way you looked at him. I saw you flirting with him."

By this time we are outside of our trailer near the apple tree in my Dad's backyard. I'm more drunk than I thought I was and I growl out, "Stop accusing me of flirting, you son of a bitch."

His hands go around my neck and I'm being choked to oblivion. I fall to the ground when he lets go and stumbles into our trailer house. I pick myself up, stumble in behind him and flop down on the couch. Harold comes out of the bedroom and carries me back in and throws me on the bed. "Don't ever call me that again. That's an insult to my mother, and no one, not even you, insults my mother."

I'm in shock the next morning. *Did that really happen?* But the bathroom mirror reveals ugly fingerprints on my neck. I feel as if I'm in a trance as we walk the few feet to my parents' house for Thanksgiving dinner. I've slathered my neck with make-up and taken great pains to cover the ugly bruises on my neck with a scarf. I'm helping Mom get dinner on the table when the scarf slips. She gasps. "What happened to your neck?"

"Harold choked me. But don't be mad at him, it was my fault. I deserved it. I said something I shouldn't have said."

Her look of disapproval says volumes, but just then Mom's brothers and their wives and children arrive for dinner and nothing more is said.

I can't wait for Thanksgiving Day to be over, so I can stop smiling and pretending to my family that everything is wonderful. Taking aspirin helps my headache but doesn't help the wound in my heart. It takes an enormous amount of energy to talk and laugh in all the right places. Harold and I leave as soon as decorum allows with the excuse that we have to pack for Denver. We are leaving on Sunday for our new adventure.

I kiss Mom good-bye at the front door as the sun is just peeping over the horizon. Dad drops us at the bus depot along with the seven boxes that contain everything we own. Sheila will be waiting for us at the bus depot in Denver and we will stay with her for a day or two until we can find our own place. Looking out the window of the bus as we pull away from the station, I'm excited at the prospects ahead. Life will be so much better there.

Oblivious to the sinister presence of something lying in wait to rule us, I lay my head on Harold's shoulder. I'm clueless about the thing that is already trying to destroy us and the members of our family, and our future generations.

Somewhere the devil is laughing.

Post Script

Life continues to be a duel between me and my many personalities. Gullible is my middle name. Optimism is the gas in my engine. When I run out of gas, I contemplate suicide.

Everything I've learned is through criticism after I've made a mistake or, if I'm lucky, I might stumble onto a correct answer. I try to read minds but that only makes me a subject of my own contempt. I read every self-help book I can afford and still it's not enough. I haven't found books that talk about inconsistent parenting, wayward children, and the adverse effects of alcohol abuse.

Virginia Satir, a famous family therapist, whom I was lucky enough to study with and know personally, used to say, "If you want to totally mess up a child to the point of mental illness, treat him/her nice one day and abuse him/her the next, said child will develop deep psychiatric problems, make terrible choices, and probably end up in prison."

I am so very grateful to God for putting her in my life, along with therapist Meryl Tullis who for several years gave me everything my mother couldn't.

My dad loved his family with all his heart and he was unaware that alcohol was the problem because it so often seemed like the solutions. And to alcoholics everyone else is the problem it is the nature of the disease. Falling into the same rut my self helps me to understand that.

My mother didn't have my resources. She also couldn't have known the abuse I'd see or that I'd be forced to leave my babies with incompetent, indifferent babysitters. Some were evil and almost killed my children, which I didn't learn about until years later.

She couldn't have known how hard I'd have to work to drag myself from the ever-burning pit of hell or how hard I'd have to work *To Be Somebody.*

Author's Note

When I started my journey as an author, I didn't have the full vision for the *Blood, Sex, and Tears* series, I now have. This book is number 4 in the series, based on the order of publication. To read my story in sequence the order is:

Just Fine Thank You
My life from a young girl through age thirteen

Dance Like There's No Tomorrow
My life as a young woman through age eighteen

To Be Somebody (Revised 2019)
My life as a young married woman through age thirty.

The next book in the series will be about my process of looking at my losses and finding serenity. I share my story from early childhood through recovery to reveal how dysfunction in families continues from one generation to another, unless there is an intentional effort to break the cycle. It's my desire that you can find hope for yourself or a loved one based on my story of redemption.

About the Author

Evelyn M. Leite, MHR, LPC professional counselor and author, has thirty-five years of experience in the addiction and mental health fields. Noted for her humanitarian work. She was inducted into the South Dakota Hall of Fame in 2008.

She is widely regarded for her seminars in counseling and education. She has designed and implemented relationship programs throughout the United States and is recognized for her success in the treatment of grief, trauma resolution, and codependency. She has authored dozens of articles, and is published by Hazelden Publications of Center City Minnesota as well as the former Johnson Institute.

In addition to this book, her best works are *Women: What Do We Want?* and *A Fix for the Family Rift Caused by Addiction*, published by Living With Solutions Press, Rapid City, South Dakota.

Your feedback is welcome!

I welcome your letters and feedback to this book please find me on Facebook under LIVING WITH SOLUTIONS or write to me at PO Box 9702, Rapid City, SD 57709

Other books by Evelyn Leite, MHR, LPC

If you enjoyed this book by Evelyn Leite, MHR, LPC, you might enjoy these, also part of the *Blood, Sex, and Tears* series:

To Be Somebody (Living With Solutions, Rapid City, SD 2014, Rev. 2019) Book 1 in the Blood, Sex, and Tears series.
ISBN: 978-1733540926

Women: What Do We Want? Changing your life is easier than you think (Living With Solutions, Rapid City, SD 2015, Rev. 2019)
ISBN: 978-1733540940

A Fix for the Rift in the Family Caused by Addiction (Living With Solutions, Rapid City, SD 2018)
Book 3 in the *Blood, Sex, and Tears* series
ISBN: 978-1733540919

Beyond the series, Evelyn offers:

Detachment (Johnson Institute Minneapolis, MN 1980, Hazelden Publications, Center City MN 1986).

Granite Island Amber Sea, Day at the Rally (Black Hills Writers Press, Rapid City, South Dakota, 2012)

A Sunday From Innocence (Black Hills Writers Press, Black Hills Literary Journal, Rapid City, South Dakota, 2013)

Available internationally through quality online retailers.

www.ingramcontent.com/pod-product-compliance
Lightning Source LLC
Chambersburg PA
CBHW030319080526
44584CB00012B/625